Twayne's United States Authors Series

Sylvia E. Bowman, *Editor*

INDIANA UNIVERSITY

William Hickling Prescott

TUSAS 251

William Hickling Prescott

WILLIAM HICKLING PRESCOTT

DONALD G. DARNELL

University of North Carolina at Greensboro

TWAYNE PUBLISHERS
A DIVISION OF G. K. HALL & CO., BOSTON

Library of Congress Cataloging in Publication Data

Darnell, Donald G.
  William Hickling Prescott.

  (Twayne's United States authors series ; TUSAS 251)
  Bibliography: p. 131 - 36.
  Includes index.
  1. Prescott, William Hickling, 1796-1859.
PS2657.D3   907'.2'024   74-26789
ISBN 0-8057-0598-8

For Jane and Sally

Contents

About the Author

Donald G. Darnell holds the M.A. degree in English from the University of Oklahoma and the Ph.D. in English from the University of Texas. He has taught at Wichita State University and the University of North Carolina at Greensboro where he is associate professor of English. His field of special interest is American literature of the nineteenth century, particularly the work of Cooper, Prescott, and Hawthorne. He has published articles in *American Literature, South Atlantic Bulletin*, and *Texas Studies in Literature and Language*. He has read papers on James Fenimore Cooper before the American Literature Section of the South Atlantic Modern Language Association.

Preface

For historians, William Hickling Prescott needs no introduction. They have long acclaimed him for his vivid narrative, careful research, and sound judgment. For the student of American literature, however, Prescott is relatively unknown, a name encountered, if at all, in discussions of his fellow Brahmins Henry Wadsworth Longfellow, James Russell Lowell, and Oliver Wendell Holmes. If for no other reason than the fact that the artistry of his histories establishes him as a literary figure of stature equal to or surpassing that of his contemporaries with whom he is most often mentioned, Prescott deserves to be better known. Thus, the purpose of this book is to provide a critical study of the work of America's most famous and popular historian, an author unsurpassed in his ability to invest historical narrative with the color, drama, and characters of romance and epic.

I have not attempted a correction of Prescott's view of historical events because doing so is not necessary. Where comment is required concerning attacks on Prescott's interpretation of Indian civilizations, I have cited the conclusions of modern historians and anthropologists, who have vindicated him. Neither have I treated Prescott's literary criticism, most of which is not important, an opinion I share with other critics. However, when his comments on other authors and historians shed light on his own work I have included them.

To illustrate the color, spectacle, and dramatic presentation of character in Prescott's work, I have drawn extensively on the histories. For Prescott's concept of his task and his aims, I have been fortunate in having before me his *Literary Memoranda*, admirably edited by C. Harvey Gardiner, the historian's recent biographer and an authority on Hispanic-American history. My debt to Professor Gardiner will be obvious. I am also indebted to the first work that surveyed and assessed Prescott's histories in detail, William Charvat and Michael Kraus's *William Hickling Prescott, Representative Selections* (1943), an excellent starting place for the study of Prescott. Acknowledgment should also be made here to David Levin's *History as Romantic Art* (1959), a basic book for any study of the Romantic historians.

I wish to thank the Research Council of the University of North Carolina at Greensboro for its support in providing me a research leave to write this book and a grant to prepare the manuscript. For their interest and assistance in this project special thanks go to Kathy Wilson Jett, Graduate Research Assistant, and Mrs. Sam P. Moore, who typed the manuscript.

DONALD G. DARNELL

University of North Carolina at Greensboro

Acknowledgments

I am indebted to J. P. Lippincott Company for permission to quote from *The Works of William Hickling Prescott*, Montezuma Edition, edited by Wilfred Harold Munro, 22 volumes, copyright 1904 by J. P. Lippincott Company.

I also wish to thank the University of Oklahoma Press for permission to quote from *The Literary Memoranda of William Hickling Prescott*, edited and with an introduction by C. Harvey Gardiner, copyright 1961 by the University of Oklahoma Press.

Quotations from *The Correspondence of William Hickling Prescott: 1833 - 1847*, transcribed and edited by Roger Wolcott, copyright 1925 by the Massachusetts Historical Society, appear through the courtesy of Houghton Mifflin Company and the Massachusetts Historical Society.

Chronology

1796   William Hickling Prescott born May 4 at Salem, Massachusetts; son of William Prescott and Catherine Hickling Prescott.

1808   Family moved to Boston, where Prescott attended private school of the Reverend Dr. John Gardiner, Rector of Trinity Church.

1811   Admitted to sophomore class at Harvard.

1812-   Accidentally blinded in left eye in dining-hall fracas at
1813   Harvard.

1814   Graduated from Harvard; entered father's law office.

1815   Inflammation of right eye caused cessation of all work. For his health, visited grandfather, Thomas Hickling, United States consul at St. Michael's in the Azores; remained there six months.

1816-   Traveled in France, Italy, and England, where Prescott con-
1817   sulted physicians about his eye. Condition, which was diagnosed as rheumatism, would plague him throughout his life.

1817   Returned to Boston; made decision to leave the law; lived at father's house and entered social life.

1820   Edited the *Club-Room*, March - July. Married Susan Amory May 4. Continued to live at father's house where his four children were born: Catherine (1824 - 29), William Gardiner (1826 - 95), Elizabeth (1828 - 64), and William Amory (1830 - 67).

1821   "Byron's Letter on Pope," review article in *North American Review*, first of many articles for journal.

1821   Decided to become man of letters; began extensive reading of French, English, and Italian literature.

1824   Began study of Spanish after listening to George Ticknor's lectures on Spanish literature.

1826 Committed himself to the writing of Spanish history: "I subscribe to the History of the Reign of Ferdinand and Isabella, January 19th, 1826." Over ten years of research and writing devoted to this first history.

1837 Published *The History of the Reign of Ferdinand and Isabella the Catholic* on Christmas Day.

1838 Elected member of American Philosophical Society, one of many honors received during lifetime.

1839 Elected member of the Royal Academy of History, Madrid.

1843 Published *The Conquest of Mexico.*

1845 Published *Biographical and Critical Miscellanies* selected from his previously published *North American Review* articles.

1845 Elected Corresponding Member of the French Institute, Academy of Moral Sciences, his "greatest academic honor." Elected member of Royal Society of Berlin.

1847 Published *The Conquest of Peru.*

1849 Began composition of *Philip the Second* on July 29.

1850 Embarked on five-month visit to England, where he was "the lion of the season." Brief visits to Paris, Brussels, and Antwerp. Awarded degree of doctor of Civil Law, Oxford, and presented at the Court of St. James as the historian of Ferdinand and Isabella.

1855 Published first two volumes of *Philip the Second.*

1856 Published *The Life of Charles the Fifth after His Abdication*, a continuation of William Robertson's *The History of the Reign of the Emperor Charles the Fifth* (1769).

1858 Suffered apoplectic stroke, February 4. Published third volume of *Philip the Second.*

1859 Died of second stroke, January 29.

1864 George Ticknor's *Life of William Hickling Prescott* published.

CHAPTER 1

The Brahmin as Historian

W HEN William Hickling Prescott died in 1859, he had completed eleven volumes of Spanish history, all written under a formidable handicap. Totally blind in one eye and his vision in the other severely impaired by acute rheumatism, Prescott composed some of his histories in almost total darkness. What led a man, the epitome of the Brahmin caste as described by Oliver Wendell Holmes, to undertake a life of intellectual rigor and physical punishment can be explained largely by the meaning of Brahminism itself; therefore, to understand William Hickling Prescott is to understand what was best in Brahminism.

I *The Brahmin Caste of New England*

Holmes defines the Brahmin caste of New England in two places, his first essay in *The Autocrat of the Breakfast Table*, published in the *Atlantic Monthly* (1857), and the first chapter of *Elsie Venner* (1861). Although the tone of each is light, an examination of the biographies and the milieu of those members making up the Brahmin caste proves the accuracy of the doctor's observations.[1] Necessary for the creation of the caste, according to Holmes, are *family* (four or five generations of colonial New England stock, preferably Massachusetts) and *money* (which secures suitable surroundings, the choicest mates, and healthy children). The product is ideally a distinct and intellectual type, slender and well made. The Brahmin is educated at Harvard, where "a congenital and hereditary" appetite for learning enables him to "take to his books as a pointer or a setter to his field-work."[2] Upon graduation, he typically travels in Europe for a year and returns to New England, usually Boston, where he makes his home. In a milieu traditionally conservative in matters social, political, and religious, he is typically a member of the Unitarian Church and of the Federalist party. He enters a profession: teaching (at Harvard), the law, or banking; he may occupy himself with investments, particularly in industries or railroads. Whatever the enterprise, the Brahmin seems destined for prominence due to a highly developed sense of noblesse oblige and a Puritan heritage — still viable beneath the Unitarianism — that requires work and achievement.

II *Family*

Prescott's credentials for membership in the Brahmin caste were unquestionable. John Prescott, the historian's ancestor, came to America about 1640, settling in Middlesex County, Massachusetts. A Puritan trained in the use of arms, he was a sturdy man who distinguished himself on several occasions in individual fights with Indians. The second- and third-generation Prescotts were officers in the Massachusetts militia and representatives of their towns in the General Court of the Colony. William Prescott (1726 - 95), grandfather of the historian, commanded American forces at Bunker Hill. His son William (1762 - 1844), father of the historian, was born on the Prescott farm at Pepperell, Massachusetts, near the present-day New Hampshire line. Upon graduation from Harvard, William Prescott taught school briefly and then entered the law. From 1789 to 1808 he had a highly successful practice at Salem, one said to be as extensive as that of Daniel Webster.[3] In 1793 he married Catherine Hickling (1767 - 1852), daughter of a wealthy Boston merchant who was later United States consul at St. Michael's in the Azores. With such admirable ancestral endowments for membership in the aristocracy of New England, William Hickling Prescott, born May 4, 1796 in Salem,[4] needed only the Boston connection to complete his list of qualifications. This need was filled in 1808 when his father moved there to invest in railroads, insurance companies, and industries — investments which also substantially increased the family wealth.

III *Education*

Young Prescott's education was typical of that given to young Brahmins who attended small, select schools taught by clergymen or aristocratic maidens. From 1808 to 1811 Prescott gathered with others of his class in the library of the Rector of Trinity Church, Boston, where he was instructed in English, Latin, and Greek by the Reverend Dr. John S. Gardiner. During these years he formed important friendships with William Howard Gardiner, the rector's son, and George Ticknor, his future biographer. According to Ticknor, Prescott as a child was bright but spoiled and willful. In the fall of 1811 he was admitted to the sophomore class at Harvard, where his performance during his first year gave no indication of the discipline and perseverance that characterized his adult life. Because it was difficult for him to study what did not immediately interest him, he gauged his study time with watch in hand, so as not to exceed it by even a minute. Classical languages, for which he had developed an early love, were his best subjects, but mathematics was hopeless for him. Having no interest in the role of scholar, Prescott was content to be the studying gentleman. He held a respectable rank in his class, for to do less would betray his tradition.

IV *New Directions*

Prescott's complacent attitude changed because of an accident that occurred during his junior year that profoundly affected his later life. As he was leaving the college dining hall one day, he was blinded in his left eye by a hard crust of bread thrown during a brawl. Prescott was taken home where he remained for several weeks. Sobered by the accident, he pursued his studies diligently upon returning to Cambridge. By the time of his graduation in August 1814, he had earned membership in Phi Beta Kappa and had been assigned a Latin poem for his exercise at commencement.

After graduation Prescott went into his father's law office, but after four or five months of study had not developed an interest in law. Again, his habits and attitude were affected by a drastic alteration in his vision. His right eye became severely inflamed and he temporarily lost sight in it as a result of acute rheumatism, a disease that would plague him throughout his life and would affect not only his eye but his neck and other joints. The attack of rheumatism in mid-January 1815 completely incapacitated Prescott, and for long periods he could neither see nor walk. When his condition had improved, doctors recommended a trip to his maternal grandfather's home in the Azores and a tour of Europe; on September 15, 1815 he sailed for St. Michael's. Following a six-month stay in the Azores he consulted physicians in London and was informed that no remedy existed for his condition; he could increase the strength of his eye only by increasing the strength of his whole system. Cautioned not to tax his weakened eye, Prescott began a gentlemanly grand tour that took him to France, Italy, back to England, and finally home to Boston in September 1817.

V   *Interlude*

With his damaged vision, a return to the law was impossible, but for a while the lack of an occupation did not trouble him. As the son of a wealthy man he did not feel — and never would — the need to earn a living. Having found a year's rest ineffective in improving the condition of his eye, Prescott turned to society. Because he was by nature quite sociable, he was soon popular in Boston. "If I were asked," a friend wrote of him later, "to name the man, whom I have known, whose coming was most sure to be hailed as a pleasant event by all whom he approached, I should not only place Prescott at the head of the list, but I could not place any other man near him." Ticknor describes Prescott at this time as one of the finest-looking men he had ever seen — "tall, well formed, manly in his bearing but gentle, with light-brown hair that was hardly changed or diminished by years, with a clear complexion and a ruddy flush on his cheek that kept for him to the last an appearance of comparative youth, but above all, with a smile that was the most absolutely contagious I ever looked upon."[5]

During this time of increased social activity Prescott met and married Susan Amory, daughter of a wealthy Boston merchant. When he was not being the social lion, Prescott found employment for his writing talents as editor and contributor to the *Club-Room*, the magazine of the social-literary club he had helped form.[6] Although the magazine was short-lived (only four issues appeared), the club itself continued for forty years and was a source of great pleasure to Prescott. Almost all requisites for the Brahmin society had been accomplished.

VI   *Choosing a Career*

With the expiration of the *Club-Room* in July 1820, Prescott had to face the serious question of what to do with his life. If Brahmin wealth made work unnecessary, Brahmin expectations nevertheless required achievement. He never questioned John Milton's dictum that "day labor" was expected of the man of talent, even though his light was denied. Furthermore, he was hard-pressed by tradition. Five generations of successful Prescotts presented a challenging moral and psychological standard to live up to. And although Prescott and his wife made their home with his parents, there is no indication that his father encouraged dependence or suggested to the son that his infirmity would excuse him from his duties. Such at least is the import of the letters the elder Prescott sent his son during the year abroad in 1816 - 17: "If your eyes will allow, I think even a very brief diary or memoranda book, containing only hints which would serve to remind you of what you have seen and heard, would prove useful. You must remember that much will be expected of you when you return. Every one will not reflect, as I do, that the great object of your visit to Europe was the recovery of health."[7]

Prescott knew that he must work, he knew that intellectual labor was congenital, but what he did not know was the form that labor would take. He had always enjoyed reading, particularly the classics, and his contributions to the *Club-Room* had whetted his appetite for writing. He decided, then, in 1821, on a career as a man of letters. To prepare himself, he undertook a detailed program of study that included principles of grammar and correct writing, the classics, and a survey of "fine prose-writers of English from Roger Ascham to the present day, principally with reference to their mode of writing, — not including historians, except as far as requisite for an acquaintance with style."[8] He supplemented these readings in English literature with a careful study of Hugh Blair's *Lectures on Rhetoric and Belles Lettres* and Lindley Murray's *English Grammar*. He spent an hour each day with the works of Tacitus, Cicero, and Livy. Since he had received good training in Latin, it was probably an enjoyable period for him.

Less than a year later, at the age of twenty-six, Prescott entered his goals in his commonplace book: "By the time I am 30, (God Willing) I propose . . . to be a *very well read English scholar,* to be acquainted with the *classical* and useful authors (prose and poetry) in *Latin, French,* and *Italian* — especially *History.*"[9] From 1822 to 1824 he undertook a vigorous study of the languages and literatures of England, France, and Italy — an ambitious undertaking considering his physical handicap and ignorance of both the language and the literature of France and Italy. His survey of French literature began with Froissart and extended to Châteaubriand; he read Montaigne and Molière, whom he made in 1828 the subject of an essay for the *North American Review.* But for the most part he found French literature less rich and vigorous than English literature. At this time he was also reading with Ticknor the *Northern Antiquities,* Thomas Percy's *Reliques,* and other romances.

His study of Italian, begun in 1823, challenged his interest more than his previous studies had and resulted in two essays about Italian literature, which were published in the *North American Review* —

one written before he found his Spanish theme and the other before
he published his first history. More important for an understanding
of his theory of historical composition were his comments on the
sixteenth-century Italian epics. The heroic poem, he observed in his
Literary Memoranda, requires *"one continued action*," the consequence being that "every thing is concentrated & refers to one event
which we keep constantly in view . . . " (I, 23 - 24). If he were to
find fault with the general plan of *Orlando Innamorato*, he would
"point out the want of some great object, & some leading personage
who might form a sort of central rallying point to the subordinate
objects & characters" (I, 44 - 45).[10] These criteria he would aim at in
his own histories.

Eye trouble and the difficulty of the language itself prevented
Prescott's study of German. He believed its mastery to be essential to
his development as a scholar, but he became discouraged and could
not pursue his other studies with his accustomed diligence.

In the autumn of 1824, however, Ticknor, now a professor of
French and Spanish literature at Harvard, began to read to Prescott
his lectures on Spanish literature. Ticknor writes that he had simply
desired to amuse his friend at a time when he was unsettled about his
future; but the lectures provided a profitable as well as pleasurable
autumn for the future historian. Prescott's *Literary Memoranda* for
November 20, 1824 lists nineteen Spanish authors to be studied, and
on December 1 he began his study of Spanish. An early progress
report, dated January 24, 1825, indicates the quality of mind and
kind of concentration Prescott possessed. "Did you never," he wrote
Ticknor, "in learning a language, after groping about in the dark for
a long while, suddenly seem to turn an angle, where the light breaks
upon you all at once? The knack seems to have come to me within
the last fortnight, in the same manner as the art of swimming comes
to those who have been splashing about for months in the water in
vain."[11] By April he had read Cervantes' *Don Quixote*, Antonio de
Solís' *Conquista de México*, the comedies of Lope de Vega and of
Calderón de la Barca, and a large number of other works in the
Spanish language.

Although Prescott's Spanish studies proceeded successfully, he
was still undecided as late as October of 1825, on the choice of a subject. "History," he had written in 1822, "has always been a favorite
study with me; and I have long looked forward to it as a subject on
which I may one day exercise my pen."[12] But the *kind* of history
remained the question. Five possibilities were considered: (1)

American history, (2) a collection of biographical sketches, (3) a history of Italian literature, (4) Roman history, and (5) Spanish history from the invasion of the Arabs to the reign of Charles V. Despite Prescott's love of Italian literature and his competence in literary history, he chose the Spanish theme. "I believe," he wrote in the *Literary Memoranda,* "the Spanish subject will be more *new* than the Italian, more *interesting* to the majority of readers, and more *useful* to me by opening another & more practical department of study. . . ."

But what probably carried greater weight in influencing his decision was the pageantry and drama of the period. "What new & interesting topics may be admitted, not forced, into the reigns of Ferdinand & Isabella?" he asks and then lists them: "the Inquisition, with its bloody persecutions, . . . — the exploits of the 'Great Captain' in Italy, a proper character for romance as well as history, — the discovery of a new world, my own country — the new policy of the monarch towards the overgrown aristocracy &c. &c" *(Memoranda, I,* 66 - 68). On January 19, 1826 he recorded his decision to write the history of the reigns of Ferdinand and Isabella.

VII   *"An Aristocrat Writing in a Democratic Age"*

Considering the man and his times, Prescott's interest in the Spanish past is not surprising. It was a more colorful age than his own, and its rulers and wars were more impressive and glorious. In contrast to Ferdinand and Isabella, there was President Polk, whom the historian described in a letter as "a mean looking individual . . . who gapes and chaws tobacco."[13] The Spanish wars to consolidate a nation and extend an empire offered an even more dramatic contrast to the Mexican War, which Prescott regarded as a sordid affair. He would not write a history of the second conquest of Mexico even when offered the papers of General Winfield Scott. "I had rather not meddle with heroes who have not been underground two centuries at least,"[14] he said in explanation of his decision. While he admired the fighting abilities of the men from the West ("They are the hardy fellows who are to break up the soil of the great western wilderness. . . . "),[15] Prescott would never, like Walt Whitman, chant the praises of the common man. He had his Brahmin suspicions of the masses and was well aware how easily they could be inflamed at political rallies where the party's orators worked their arts. "The good sense of the people," he noted, was a phrase with "more humbug in it than [he] once thought."[16]

In this distrust of the political sense of the common man, Prescott shared the attitudes of his caste. Like his Federalist father, he belonged to the conservative school of politics. He knew there was little likelihood of a return to the values of George Washington and Alexander Hamilton. Consequently he would never involve himself in politics or understand its appeal for others. "Why," he queried his friend and fellow historian George Bancroft, "do you coquet with such a troublesome termagant as politics, when the glorious Muse of History opens her arms to receive you?"[17]

Prescott was no less alienated from the business world, which was more foreign to him than the Mexico he never saw. In a letter to a German friend, he accurately analyzed his own position: "A person in our country who takes little interest in politicians or in making money — our staples you know — will be thrown pretty much on his own resources, and if he is not fond of books he may as well go hang himself. . . . "[18]

"An aristocrat writing in a democratic age," as Michael Kraus describes him,[19] Prescott found the world outside his own circle to be an alien one, and for a man lacking his intellectual vigor, the Brahmin milieu could have become only a haven. But for Prescott, that milieu provided ideal working and living conditions. If it was insular, for Prescott it was also all-sufficient, providing clubs, friends, and the families where his children might find their mates.

Nor was there a need to travel. Prescott money and connections brought the necessary books and manuscripts from the libraries of Europe and Mexico. Prescott's world was Boston and, aside from a few brief trips to New York City, Albany, and Washington and his four-month visit in England, he never left it except for his seasonal sojourns to the family home at Pepperell and for trips to Nahant and Lynn, Massachusetts.

For literary work, Prescott could not have had a more congenial atmosphere, for he could number among his friends some of the leading literary figures of the day — Henry Wadsworth Longfellow, Ticknor, Jared Sparks, and George Bancroft. They supported and praised one another's efforts and were reluctant to make adverse criticism in print. "I had rather write a quire in manuscript than print a word that should harm or displease a friend,"[20] Prescott wrote apropos of a possible review of Sparks' *Washington*. Prescott's world, then, was a gentlemanly one of good books, good clubs, good manners, and love of letters for their own sake.

Given this environment and ease of circumstances, Prescott could construct a life for himself that admitted neither intellectual nor professional compromises. "I shall never be satisfied to do my work slovenly or superficially," he wrote in his *Literary Memoranda*. "It would be impossible for me to do the job-work of a literary hack. Fortunately I am not driven to write for *bread* and I will never write for money" (II, 10). His choice of career, subject, and way of life Prescott never regretted. On his forty-ninth birthday and twenty-fifth wedding anniversary, he acknowledged the significant influences on his life: "Family, friends, and fortune, — these have furnished me materials for enjoyment greater and more constant than is granted to most men." To this list he added books, "the love of letters . . . which has proved my solace . . . under afflictions mental and bodily. . . ."[21] More revealing of the character of the man is the entry in the *Memoranda* for June 26, 1836: "I met with a remark of Dr. Johnson on Milton, at an early period, stating that the poet gave up his history of Britain, on becoming blind, since no one could pursue such investigations under such disadvantages. This remark of the great doctor confirmed me in the resolution to attempt the contrary" (I, 191). Having made his decision, Prescott undertook a career that he knew from his own experience and from the warnings of his physicians would jeopardize his remaining vision. As it turned out, he was able to work until his death.

Considered apart from his literary labors, Prescott's life was singularly uneventful in comparison to that of his contemporaries in the profession of letters. He had no affiliation with a college as did Sparks, Ticknor, and Longfellow; no involvement in politics and government as did Edward Everett and George Bancroft; no involvement in litigation or wars with the press as did James Fenimore Cooper; nor did he ever take residence in the lands he described in his works, as did Washington Irving. In Prescott's domestic and social life, a marvelous order existed. Until 1845 (and for twenty-five years of his marriage), he made his home with his parents on Bedford Street. At his father's death in 1845, Prescott, with his wife, mother, and children, moved to a house on Beacon Street, where he lived for thirteen years until his death. Wherever the residence, the household revolved around Prescott's working schedule and his social commitments during his leisure. In his wife Susan, Prescott had an excellent companion who disliked traveling even more than he and who was content to make a quiet life for her family in Boston.

For a man constantly concerned about his health, Prescott led a remarkably active social life. According to his close friend William

Gardiner, no man "had a keener zest of social enjoyment in all its varieties."[22] In addition to his writing and social activity, Prescott was also concerned with his civic responsibilities. He used his money and prestige to improve the cultural life of Boston and help the unfortunate. According to Rollo Ogden, Prescott regularly gave away one-tenth of his income to charity. For ten years he was an active trustee of the Asylum for the Blind, and he served with George Ticknor as a trustee of the Boston Athenaeum. As important as social life and community service were to Prescott, though, true personal satisfaction lay in his historical labors. One of the many entries in the *Memoranda*, commenting on his choice of a career, is worth citing: "January 11, 1846. *I am satisfied I am never so happy — present & in retrospection — as when heartily engaged in the vocation, which I may call my destiny.* Heartily engaged in this, life will glide like a pleasant dream — & yet, with the blessing of Heaven, leave something more than a dream in the substantial fruits of it" (II, 163).

VIII *Stature*

Prescott's prediction of substantial fruits came true in his own lifetime in the publication of eleven volumes of history, which were translated into five languages, and in a one-volume collection of biographical and critical miscellanies.[23] There was, however, a long wait before the first harvest. Beginning in 1826, he worked for nearly twelve years before *The History of the Reign of Ferdinand and Isabella the Catholic* was published. Because he was preeminently a social man and also knew himself to be indolent by nature, he imposed upon himself a rigorous discipline and writing schedule. To guarantee that he would produce a set number of pages by a deadline (his own, never his publisher's), he sometimes made a bond with his reader-secretary to pay him a specified sum (once a thousand dollars) if he did not complete a certain number of pages by a specified time. When he completed the history on June 25, 1836, he was reluctant to publish it immediately, desiring to keep it for emendations and additions. A remark by his father that a man who writes a book he is afraid to publish is a coward put an end to his hesitation, and a search for a publisher was immediately begun. The American Stationers' Company of Boston agreed to print 1,250 copies, with the expectation of selling them within five years. In England, Prescott's agent, Colonel Thomas Aspinwall, made a contract with Richard Bentley to publish the work.

Ferdinand and Isabella appeared in Boston on Christmas Day

1837 and enjoyed a tremendous success. Within a few months the 1,250 copies printed to supply the market for five years were sold out. The book's popular success was matched by the critical reception given it by scholars in the field of Spanish history. Prescott could count on favorable reviews and comments from his friends Sparks, Bancroft, and Gardiner (who reviewed it for the *North American Review*), but the authorities on Spanish history and Arab history would have to decide the book's permanent scholarly reputation. With few exceptions, their reviews were laudatory. Prescott's reputation as a competent historian was established with his first work, a reputation he embellished with the succession of histories that followed.

Besides bringing Prescott public acclaim, the histories were also the means of opening correspondence with some of the outstanding scholars and writers of his day, among whom were the Swiss historian Jean Charles Sismondi, by whom Prescott had been influenced in his own writing; the Count Adolphe de Circourt, the author of a five-installment review of *Ferdinand and Isabella* in the *Bibliothèque Universelle de Genève*; Pascual de Gayangos, an authority on the Spanish Arabs, who reviewed Prescott's first history and later became his most valuable aide abroad; Baron Alexander von Humboldt, the German geographer of Mexico; Thomas Babington Macaulay; Washington Irving; and Maria Edgeworth. Nor was more formal recognition of Prescott's achievement slow in coming. In his selective list of the "more considerable" honors Prescott received during his lifetime, Ticknor includes over twenty-eight honorary degrees and memberships in honorary societies. But the most prestigious were, in Prescott's estimation, the Royal Academy of History, Madrid (1839); The French Institute, Academy of Moral Sciences (1845); The Royal Society of Berlin (1845); and the Doctor of Civil Laws, Oxford, England (1850).

The culmination of Prescott's public honors came in 1850 during his visit to England. During this period he was at work on *Philip the Second*, but the writing was not going well. He was now fifty-four, and as his health had not been good, a change of scene and rest from his literary labors seemed advisable. Accompanied by his reader-secretary John Foster Kirk, Prescott arrived in England on June 3, 1850, where he soon became, in Ticknor's words, "the lion of the season." Included among the highlights of his visit were attendance at the Ascot Races, dinner at Sir Robert Peel's, visits to country houses and castles, an introduction to the Duke of Wellington, conversations with Macaulay and Benjamin Disraeli, ceremonies at Oxford where he received the Doctor of Civil Laws degree, and presentation at the Court of St. James as the historian of Ferdinand and Isabella.

After his return to Boston, reinvigorated by his travels and encouraged by his honors, Prescott resumed work on *Philip the Second*, finishing the first two volumes in 1854. In February 1858, while completing the third volume, he suffered a stroke of apoplexy that left him bedridden for several days and unable to walk without assistance for several more. His strength, slow to return, never reached the level he had maintained before the attack. In September of that year he returned to some light literary activity, preparing additions and emendations for a future edition of *The Conquest of Mexico*. He had begun to think seriously of returning to concentrated work on *Philip the Second*, and on January 27 of the new year he talked of it as a real possibility. The next morning he suffered a fatal apoplectic stroke.

Before burial in the family tomb under St. Paul's Church, Prescott's body, in accord with his earlier request, was placed for a while in his library where he had gathered the books and manuscripts from which he constructed his histories.

CHAPTER 2

The Scholar Gentleman

PRESCOTT'S entry into the field of Spanish history with the publication of *The History of the Reign of Ferdinand and Isabella the Catholic* in 1838 could not have occurred at a more propitious time. Interest in Spain and Spanish subjects was running high, and the opening of the Spanish archives had made available to Prescott the books and manuscripts unknown or forbidden to his predecessors in the field.[1] He capitalized on these opportunities, establishing with his first history a reputation that opened other libraries and private collections on the Continent to him, as well as securing the assistance of scholars throughout Europe in collecting the materials for his subsequent histories.

In these sources and those he had used for his first history, Prescott found the documents that enabled him to maintain an authentic and colorful narrative throughout four multivolume works, *The History of the Reign of Ferdinand and Isabella the Catholic* (1838), *The History of the Conquest of Mexico* (1843), *The History of the Conquest of Peru* (1847), and *The History of Philip the Second, King of Spain* (1855 - 58). His diligence in gathering material from these sources was matched in his composition of the histories by an impressive display of ingenuity and power of concentration that overcame a formidable physical handicap. These qualities, along with his commitment to the Spanish theme, his desire to distinguish himself, and the personal wealth that provided the time and materials necessary for the writing, contributed in no small way to Prescott's continuing reputation as America's foremost historian of the Spanish Empire.

I *Interest in Spain*

Characterized at first by Puritan hostility toward Catholicism, American interest in Spain began early. In 1699 Cotton Mather had learned Spanish in order to translate "a little Body of the *Protestant Religion*" for the inhabitants of Spanish America.[2] Soon, however, the desire to advance the Protestant faith was replaced by a desire to advance trade between the two nations. The Peninsular Campaign of Wellington against the French had focused America's and the world's attention on the Spanish land and its people. By the 1830s interest in Spain, particularly her past, had grown considerably. Robert Southey, whom Prescott regarded as an authority on Spain, had drawn on the Spanish past for his own work, *Roderick the Last of the Goths* (1814) and for his translations, *Amadis of Gaul* (1803) and *The Cid* (1808). In America the Spanish conquests of Mexico and Peru were recognized as rich sources for literary exploitation, something not to be lost sight of in a new country lacking a romantic past. William Gilmore Simms had written *The Vision of Cortes* in 1829, and Robert Montgomery Bird had used both Mexico and Peru as settings for *Orallossa* (1832), *Calavar or the Knight of the Conquest* (1834), and *The Infidel or The Fall of Mexico* (1835).

In addition to those themes associated with the conquests — chivalry, exploration, battles, and the destruction of pagan civilizations — another theme, the concept of the noble savage, dear to American artists and audiences of the early nineteenth century, was inevitably linked to the encounter between the two cultures. Portrayed as forgiving, loyal, and self-sacrificing, the Indian destroyed by his contact with Europeans was already a popular literary type by the late eighteenth century. The German playwright August von Kutzebue glorified him in *The Virgin of the Sun* (1791) and *Pizarro in Peru* (1795), both of which were performed in America in 1800.

Yet another bond between the United States and Spain was the former's interest in the factual and mythical Columbus. Early poetic treatments of his story had appeared in Philip Freneau's *The Pictures of Columbus* (1774) and Joel Barlow's *The Vision of Columbus* (1787), which was greatly expanded as *The Columbiad* in 1807. But until the nineteenth century little was known about the discoverer of America. Then in 1825 Martín Fernández de Navarrete began publishing his editions of the records of the Spanish maritime discovery of America. Soon afterward, Washington Irving, in Spain from 1826 to 1829, drew on Navarrete's work when he wrote in 1828 *The Life and Voyages of Columbus*, followed three years later by *The Companions of Columbus*.

The time was ripe for Prescott's entry into the field of Spanish history. He had waited almost too long, since Irving's *Conquest of Granada*, published in 1829, and the earlier Columbus volumes had, by Prescott's own admission, deprived of their novelty his treatment of the two most significant events in the reign of Ferdinand and Isabella. But with interest in Spain still strong, increased, in fact, by Irving's popular treatment of Spanish history and his use of Spanish legends in *The Alhambra* (1832), Prescott could afford to be patient. As a historian and thorough, conscientious researcher, he had advantages that placed him above his New York competitor. He also had advantages over his predecessors in the field, as the early decades of the nineteenth century witnessed the publication of manuscripts and histories, both general and specialized, that were germane to his study of the Spanish empire.

II *Sources*

Until Prescott's entry into the field, the best-known historian of Spain was the Scottish historian, William Robertson (1721 - 93), author of the *The History of the Reign of Charles the Fifth* (1769) and *The History of the Discovery and Settlement of America* (1777). In *Charles the Fifth*, which described Spain during the height of her power, the author did not trace her rise to that position. Consequently, there was a definite need for an account of the consolidation of Castile and Aragon, the defeat of the Moors, and the discovery of the New World. The *History of America*, a study of Spain in the New World, was widely read in America and serialized in American periodicals. For a hundred years, according to Stanley T. Williams, it helped make fashionable the numerous prose and verse narratives concerning Mexico and South America. Prescott and Irving had read it, and before them, Joel Barlow had drawn on it for *The Vision of Columbus*.

Robertson's history suffered, however, from a defect common to all Spanish histories written before the nineteenth century — lack of manuscript sources.[3] Since the Inquisition made men reluctant to write, much less publish, a large amount of material pertinent to Spanish history had remained in manuscript during the sixteenth, seventeenth, and eighteenth centuries. If manuscripts were collected, they were too often incorrectly cataloged — if at all — and were placed in archives closed to native, as well as foreign, scholars. This situation changed in 1780 with the opening of the Spanish archives, and scholars began researches which culminated in the 1820s and 30s with the publication of specialized histories and collections of manuscripts invaluable to the vast theme Prescott undertook.

Before he could become a historian, Prescott had to become a conscientious collector of books and manuscripts. He not only needed the new materials that were appearing during the golden age of research in Spanish history but also the works of his predecessors in the field and the sources they had used. In Ticknor he had a friend with a good library from which he borrowed heavily during his exploratory reading in Spanish subjects. But for the kind of history he wanted to undertake, even the resources of the best domestic libraries were inadequate. Commenting on the Boston Athenaeum in 1828, Prescott wrote: "It falls somewhat heavy upon a writer here, that he must make a collection for himself of such works as in other countries are already prepared for him in the public libraries."[4] Some books simply were not available, in either the United States or abroad. However difficult it might be to find books in Europe, that was still the place Prescott had to search for his materials. Since he was looking particularly for manuscripts, the problem was even more difficult.

III   *Agents and Archives*

The story of amassing the collection of books and manuscripts necessary for Prescott's histories rivals in interest the collection itself. Because his "good" eye was affected by changes in light and temperature, Prescott would not travel to Europe to consult with scholars or visit libraries; furthermore, the condition of his eye made ca.eful scrutiny of old records and script impossible, and copying a manuscript written in a foreign language was out of the question. Also, the periodic attacks of rheumatism he suffered throughout his life made travel unwise. Finally, Prescott was fond of the creature comforts — good friends, Madeira wine, family — the Brahmin world, in a word; and he refused to leave it. He made only two trips to Europe, neither for purposes of research: one for his health in 1815, before he began studying history, and a five-month pleasure trip in 1850. Between these dates, three of his histories appeared, all compiled from material drawn from European collections. How Prescott was able to accomplish this without setting foot in Europe is explained as much by the intellectual climate of the age as by the personality and financial condition of the man himself.

materials for the historian. Pascual de Gayangos, a Spanish scholar of the Arabic period in Spain, wrote while living in England a complimentary review of *Ferdinand and Isabella* for the *Edinburgh Review*.[6] Writing Gayangos to thank him for his review, Prescott asked the young scholar if he had any materials pertaining to Cortés and Pizarro that he might share. Gayangos' affirmative answer began a relationship that proved of immeasurable value to Prescott, for Gayangos not only sent Prescott copies of his papers but also agreed to search the public and private archives of Europe for the historian. In England he complied an index of materials pertaining to Philip II in the British Museum and supervised copying manuscripts from the collection of Sir Thomas Phillipps, which was regarded by Sparks as the largest private collection in the world.[7]

A bibliographer and linguist, as well as a scholar, Gayangos possessed the precise qualities Prescott needed in an aide: Gayangos knew his way around in archives and he could catch mistakes in the copyists' transcription of a foreign language, a not infrequent occurrence. He found that in England, documents written in French could not be entrusted to English copyists and that in Spain the copyists could not read old Spanish. As a scholar himself, he was sensitive to the kind of materials Prescott was interested in and frequently anticipated the historian's needs. Equally important in a time of ignorance, inefficiency, and petty graft in the administration of archives, he was shrewd and patient — qualities which were sorely tested during his search of the archives at Simancas, the repository of the royal Spanish papers of state during Philip II's reign. Some thirty million documents, letters, and private reports had been gathered into eighty thousand packages and deposited without order or index in the fifty-room former castle of the Admiral of Castile. If by chance an employee happened to find a requested document, the visitor was not allowed to copy it or to make notes, extracts, or even summaries. With that regulation suspended by his petition to the minister, Gayangos next found himself handicapped by a sixteen-hour work week, owing to the number of religious holidays and limited open hours. Despite these obstacles, his search was exceptionally fruitful. Prescott could not have been better served; even if his sight had been perfect and his health robust, he could not have matched by a third the industry, shrewdness, and patience of Gayangos.

Dependent as Prescott was on his aides, he was not a passive participant in the gathering of the source materials for his histories. He knew where the materials were and sent long letters with specific in-

structions for obtaining what he wanted. He coordinated the efforts
of his researchers and aides and kept them posted on each other's
progress. Prescott was also a persistent and shameless asker of favors.
When a complete stranger, a Catholic monk at Palermo, wrote
criticizing his vocabulary in *Ferdinand and Isabella,* Prescott
answered with a request that he use his influence on Cortés' descen-
dant, also a resident of Palermo, to allow copies to be made of any
papers bearing on the conquistador. His oddest request, however,
was the one he made of William Miller, an English soldier of fortune
and former general in the army of Peru who had been banished from
Peru in 1839 and was not allowed to return for twenty years:
"Should you again take up your residence in Peru and be at leisure
to think of other peoples' hobbies," Prescott wrote Miller in August
1840, "you will greatly oblige me by trying to get any copies of
original manuscripts, of whatever kind relating to the first Conquest
of Peru, Quito and Chile. . . ."[8]

Each shipment of books and manuscripts from the Continent was
an addition to an already impressive collection of Spanish materials.
By 1845 Prescott's library numbered four to five thousand volumes.
Since the particular history he was writing determined what
materials were necessary, the library grew in four stages. As would
be expected, the reigns of the Spanish monarchs required more
material than the two conquests with their narrower scope: the
catalog of Prescott's library contains twenty-two pages of books
relating to *Ferdinand and Isabella,* twenty-six relating to *Philip the
Second,* and eight relating to the two conquests.[9] In addition to the
printed materials there were the manuscript collections which enor-
mously increased the value of the library and guaranteed the quality
of scholarship in the histories. (Roger Bigelow Merriman later used
the books and manuscripts collected by Prescott for *Ferdinand and
Isabella* for the first two volumes of his definitive *Rise of the Spanish
Empire in the Old World and in the New* [1918 - 1934]) For *The
Conquest of Mexico* Prescott accumulated over five thousand pages
of manuscript; his collection of manuscripts for *Peru* was fuller and
more complete. The real wealth of his holdings, however, lay in his
materials for the reign of Philip II, some 370 books and twenty-five
folio manuscript volumes bearing directly on Philip and his times.

IV   *Handicap and Discipline*

The task of converting the information from books, manuscripts,
documents, and letters into written history proved difficult for two

reasons: Prescott's congenital laziness and his impaired vision. Once he was writing, Prescott enjoyed his work. The difficulty was to get going. That he recognized his tendency to be dilatory can be seen in the self-admonitions of his memoranda: "Eleven months will have elapsed since my completion of the *History of the Conquest*," and in another place, "*Horresco!* I have actually done nothing since last entry. What the deuce is the matter. Is it the lazy Beacon St. atmosphere. Fie on it! If I can once get in harness — & at work, I shall do well — but my joints are stiff, I think, as I grow old." He realized, however, what his work meant to him: "A miracle — have kept my resolve — thus far — & been industrious three whole days! . . . I am convinced my recipe for happiness lies in the active exercise of my powers in literary pursuits."[10]

Prescott established a schedule and regimen to regulate his workday and also to strengthen his eye by improving the overall tone of his body. He determined to rise early and agreed to pay a forfeit to the servant who knocked at his door if he failed to rise immediately. After an early morning horseback ride and breakfast with his family, Prescott met with his reader in the study for three hours of uninterrupted work. A two-mile walk before and again after dinner was followed by another two hours of work, after which Prescott joined his wife in the library, where she read to him before they retired. Prescott faithfully exercised, despite any physical discomfort that might accompany his activity. If there was a storm or if the glare from the snow on a sunny day was too bright, he would wrap up and walk vigorously about the coldest parts of the house or saw and chop firewood under cover. Frequently his rheumatism made this regimen painful, but he persisted, since he believed that the exercise helped his eye.

While Prescott's overall health was improved by this program, the eye never had sufficient strength for the intensive reading and writing necessary for the composition of history. Although he had hoped the vision in the eye might improve, he realized in time that he must be content to guard jealously the sight that remained, rationing it by the minute. He was never totally blind and, according to Ticknor, could always recognize the features of his friends. Nor was he completely shut off from the books in his library. There were, in fact, a few periods when he actually enjoyed good vision. "My eyes have been uniformly in excellent condition," he wrote in August 1836, "permitting a free use of them from four to five hours, indeed as much time as I desired every day." Ticknor reports that

Prescott was able to read with considerable regularity while he worked on *The Conquest of Mexico*. But these periods were the exception.[11] He used his eye very little in the preparation of *Ferdinand and Isabella* and even less in his work on *Philip the Second*, which was written during the latter part of his life when his eye was in its worst condition. Even in the beginning he paid for the slightest strain on the eye with the loss of a week's work. From 1846 until his death he measured his reading vision in lengths of ten and thirty minutes a day, with considerable intervals of rest between. Even when the exceptions are noted, it is obvious that Prescott did not have vision of sufficient strength and duration to write his histories unaided.

To offset this handicap, for over thirty years he employed a series of reader-secretaries. There were ten of them, all recent Harvard graduates (with one exception). Each had a knowledge of foreign languages.[12] While a few served only a year or two, the average length of service was three to four years; but John Foster Kirk, Prescott's last reader, was with him eleven years. The remuneration and requirements for the position were spelled out in a letter Prescott wrote to George Bancroft. If the reader agreed to work for at least a minimum of three years, he would receive $250 a year for a six-hour day six-day work week. He should know the French and Spanish languages not "as a critic or scholar, but as a gentleman; in short, well enough to read the common writers of history, &c. with ease."[13] The salary increased to $400 and $450 during the last ten years of Prescott's career. Fortunately the quality of his readers improved sooner. "I began," Prescott notes in the *Memoranda*, "with teaching a reader to pronounce the Spanish so that I could comprehend him, and in this way went thro' several quartos, of which my reader himself understood no more than he did of the Chaldaic" (I, 191). This early reader was in great contrast to Henry Cheever Simonds, his reader from 1831 to 1835, who read with the "right emphasis" the Latin, Spanish, French, Italian, and English authors in Prescott's library. In readers such as Simonds, Kirk, James Lloyd English, and Edmund Otis, Prescott was very fortunate; they gave him good service, in addition to leaving an intimate view of the historian's working methods.

V *Memory and Composition*

English, Prescott's reader from 1827 to 1831, has described in detail a typical working week and the conditions under which he and the historian worked. Because Prescott's eye was extremely sensitive to variations in light early in his career, it was necessary to regulate carefully the amount of illumination in the study. Even the passing of a cloud made it necessary to adjust the window curtains. With his back to the curtained window, Prescott sat facing a green screen while his reader sat behind him and to the left beneath the one window in the room that was not partially or wholly darkened.

Crucial as proper lighting was to the health of his eye and for reading, Prescott required no light at all for writing. While on his grand tour in London in 1816, he purchased a writing apparatus for the blind. This instrument, called a noctograph, consisted of a ten-inch by nine-inch frame crossed by sixteen stout parallel brass wires folded down on a sheet of carbon paper which covered a sheet of writing paper. The frame held the two sheets in contact, and the wires guided the writer's ivory stylus, the pressure of which on the carbon paper left indelible writing on the paper beneath. This instrument was an obvious boon to a blind person since there was no longer any worry about writing over what had been previously written or determining whether the pen was dry. But there were serious drawbacks. Since it was impossible to see what had been written, one could not go back and make corrections for fear of making the manuscript illegible. The writer could only go forward and make his corrections after the point where the mistake had occurred. Even more frustrating were Prescott's experiences in writing a good page and finding that he had not inserted a page of writing paper beneath the carbon. Despite these disadvantages, the noctograph was invaluable to Prescott, for he hated to compose by dictation and refused to do it if the work were intended for publication. Without the noctograph, the histories, if they had been written at all, would probably have been very different.

The effect of the noctograph on Prescott's style becomes apparent upon examination of his method of composition. With his reader-secretary seated behind him reading from a book or a manuscript, Prescott would listen and call out "mark that" when a passage struck him as significant. At the same time Prescott himself took notes on the noctograph as the reader read. The reader then copied the marked passages and Prescott's noctograph notes in a very large, legible script. Prescott then had these copies read to him or, if his eye permitted, read them himself. Next came the process of assimilating the materials. Prescott would have the copious notes read to him six to sometimes a dozen times to impress them on his memory. He would then spend several days preparing the chapter in his mind, memorizing not only the content but also the positions of sentences and paragraphs in the chapter. "My way has been lately," he records in the *Memoranda*, "to go over a large mass in my mind — over & over — till ready to throw it on paper — *then* an effort rather of memory than creation. — Thus I make all the retrenchment, & other alterations in my mind — which saves my eyes — & the writing process is done in a jiffy" (II, 80). The first and second chapters of the fifth book of *The Conquest of Peru*, equaling fifty-six pages of print, he memorized before starting to write. He later complained that his memory was failing him when he could hold only forty printed pages of *Philip the Second* in his mind. When he tried to write extemporaneously — that is, without memorizing — he was unsuccessful (*Memoranda*, II, 92).

With the division or chapter memorized, Prescott began to write rapidly on the noctograph, dashing off sheets which his reader began to copy. If synonymous phrases or parallel forms of speech occurred to him in the process, he wrote them down along with the original rather than halting the flow of composition by pausing to determine the better choice. The tempo was fast, aided at times by Prescott's humming, as he worked on the battle scenes, "O give me but my Arab steed!" When Prescott had finished the chapter, the secretary read the copied noctograph pages to him, and Prescott began the process of careful correction and revision. After the chapter had been corrected, it was again copied by the secretary in a large, heavy handwriting and read this time by Prescott himself. Sometimes, because of the condition of his eye, he could give only a few minutes to this task each day, but he felt it essential that he see the material himself before it went to the press. The effect of memorizing a chapter, of thoroughly mastering the content and form of his material, could not have failed to affect the style of the composition. Ticknor says it gave a freshness and freedom to Prescott's thoughts and to his mode of expression. Considering the formal quality of Prescott's prose, this statement has to be accepted with reservation; however, Ticknor's view that memorizing affected the flow and cadence of Prescott's sentences seems accurate.

Prescott's wealth, assistants, extensive manuscript collections, excellent memory, and painstaking care in the preparation of his texts contributed greatly to the quality and style of his works. Yet important as these factors were in creating memorable history, they must be weighed along with Prescott's carefully considered historical point of view and with his theory of historical composition.

CHAPTER 3

Point of View

I am at a loss what to admire most in your work," Pascual de Gayangos wrote Prescott in 1839, "whether your exquisite erudition and extensive reading, or your profound philosophy, — or that most difficult as well as most rare quality in an historian — freedom from all political as well as religious bias."[1] It is interesting that this list includes the qualities Prescott himself considered essential for a historian: he must be strictly impartial and love truth and declare it under all circumstances and at all hazards. He must be conversant not only with the laws, constitution, and general resources of the people he is depicting but also with "the nicer moral and social relations, the informing spirit which gives life to the whole." He must be able to transport himself to other ages and nations and get the "very form and pressure of the times he is delineating." He must be accurate in his geography and chronology. Finally, the historian "must display the various powers of a novelist or dramatist, throwing his characters into suitable lights and shades, disposing his scenes so as to awaken and maintain an unflagging interest, and diffusing over the whole that finished style without which his work will only become a magazine of materials for the more elegant edifices of subsequent writers." These criteria, which appeared in Prescott's review (1829) of Irving's *Conquest of Granada*,[2] show that he developed early in his career a theory of historical writing that gave equal weight to research and literary craftsmanship. Because this theory coincided ideally with his historical point of view, his success and stature as an historian were significantly affected.[3]

I *Influences*

One of the major influences that affected Prescott's point of view as a historian was eighteenth-century Rationalism. An outgrowth of the influence of John Locke, René Descartes, and Francis Bacon, Rationalism rejected the traditional Christian concept of miracles and wonders as the shaping forces of history. Believing that the universe operated according to natural law, the Rationalist emphasized scientific investigation of cause and effect to explain events and patterns. When the Rationalist historians, in turn, adopted this viewpoint and began to examine in their works climate, geography, society, commerce, and industry, they thereby broadened considerably the field of history. Further, since a scientific spirit of investigation pervaded their approach to history, it was natural that the Rationalist historians would be hostile to superstition or anything else that seemed to hinder freedom of inquiry. Consequently, religion came to be regarded as an inhibiting force, not only preventing the quest for knowledge but also keeping man in subjugation and fear. The attitude, then, of the Rationalist historian toward religion was typically skeptical. He denied the fall of man and the efficacy of the church to improve man's lot; instead, he believed in progress and man's ability to reach perfection by the use of his reason.

Prescott was familiar with the works of the Rationalist historians. Voltaire, Montesquieu, Edward Gibbon, and Robertson he studied carefully, commenting perceptively on their merits and faults. As an intellectual and a university-trained man of the nineteenth century, he could respond to the Rationalistic approach to history. As a Unitarian he could appreciate the Rationalists' attack on superstition and coercive religious beliefs. He admired Voltaire both for his method of historical composition and for his concern for freedom: "Nowhere is his invective more keenly directed than against acts of cruelty and oppression, — above all, religious oppression."[4]

But Prescott's own religious beliefs — his belief in a benevolent deity, in New Testament ethics, and in immortality — made the skepticism of the Rationalists unacceptable. Voltaire's skepticism, he found, had a pernicious effect: in his histories "the most momentous events are traced to the most insignificant causes, and the ripest schemes of wisdom are shown to have been baffled by the intervention of the most trivial accidents. Thus, the conduct of the world seems to be regulated by chance; the springs of human action are resolved into selfishness; and religion, of whatever denomination, is only a different form of superstition."[5]

Gibbon was guilty of the same charge. Although an accomplished writer possessing learning "fully equal to his vast subject," the

English historian was lacking in good faith. In his chapter on the progress of Christianity he had by "a style of innuendo . . . contrived, with Iago-like duplicity, to breathe a taint of suspicion on the purity which he dares not openly assail."[6] Neither Voltaire nor Gibbon exhibited in their writing "a generous moral sentiment." Nor could Prescott accept the lack of moral enthusiasm in their writings. To contemplate the "martyr who suffers for conscience's sake . . . with the smile, or rather the sneer of Philosophic indifference is to relinquish one of the most powerful engines for the movement of human passion, which is never so easily excited as by deeds of suffering, self-devoted heroism."[7] Sensibility in history, as well as in art, was important.

Man's perfectibility by reason, a doctrine dear to the Rationalist, was equally difficult for Prescott to accept. Historically, the excesses of the French Revolution had rung the death knell of that concept, at least as far as Prescott and other Federalists were concerned. We have already noted Prescott's attitude toward the masses and their susceptibility to the forensic powers of the political orators. Finally, there was probably too much dormant Puritanism or maybe New England common sense in the historian to take the perfectibility of man as a valid assumption. Despite these differences, Rationalism, particularly as it is reflected in the works of the Rationalist historians, had an important influence on Prescott. Their careful examination of cause and effect and their attention to environment, culture, government, and races Prescott adopted and combined with ideas and techniques of historical composition current in his own day, to produce a form of history unique in America.

Although Prescott was strongly influenced by the Rational school of history, his concern for literary craftsmanship and the treatment of particular themes linked him more closely with the school of Romanticist historians. A major reason for his affinity with this later school was its concept of an organic and evolutionary universe, a contrast to the mechanistic, static cosmos envisioned by the Rationalists. Harry E. Barnes, in *A History of Historical Writing*, writes of the Romanticist school and the theories that dominated it:

The underlying historical premise of the historiography of Romanticism was the doctrine of the gradual and unconscious nature of cultural evolution in any nation. The Romanticists proclaimed the organic unity and unique development of all forms of national culture. There was a decidedly mystical strain in their thinking which maintained that these unconscious creative

forces move and operate in a mysterious manner which defies direct intellectual analysis. . . . Without giving any scientific explanation of the development of the spirit of a nation, they attributed the peculiarities of national institutions, laws, literature and government to the "genius" of the nation,
and then represented national character as the product of the art, literature,
laws, and institutions of a people.[8]

Closely related to these theories were two concepts held by the
English and American Romantic historians concerning the Anglo-
Saxon's superior capacity for government and the existence of an in-
nate libertarian impulse, or "gene," in the Germanic people. The
two became combined in what Barnes terms "a rudimentary 'Ger-
manism' — the derivation of all important European races from the
'Goths,' and the weaving in of Anglo-Saxon history as a subordinate
incident of Gothic triumph."[9]

Prescott's views coincided with these theories of the Romantic
school. He accepted without question the superiority of the Anglo-
Saxon's political capacity, and he believed that the Germanic
"gene" was innately libertarian, vigorous, and energetic.[10] As an
American living in an age when the movement toward full political
liberty and equality had reached a climax, he could not do otherwise
than believe in the spirit of a nation. Finally, there was something
almost mystical in his conception of historical causation. He saw the
universe as evolutionary but directed by a divine providence that
ordered its operation according to moral, as well as natural, laws.
Inseparable from this conception was Prescott's belief in progress
which he regarded as evolutionary, moral, and natural. The
progressive principle became, in effect, his touchstone for evaluating
men, institutions, and nations and served as the common
denominator of his concept of a nation's spirit, racial "gene," and
democracy.

Prescott's commitment to the democratic principle, heightened by
a nineteenth-century American sense of destiny, significantly influenced his point of view as an historian. He possessed, in David
Levin's words, a belief in America's "unique situation as the country
most nearly in harmony with divine (or natural) laws."[11] This meant
that it was also the country that most closely coincided with the
progressive principle. "It is curious," Prescott wrote in his review of
Bancroft's *United States*, "to observe how steadily the progress of
freedom, civil and religious, — of the enjoyment of those rights
which may be called the natural rights of humanity, — has gone on

from east to west. . . ."[12] America, then, was symbol and fact of man's progress toward religious, intellectual, and political freedom. Furthermore, this progress was divinely ordered: "It was a fortunate, or, to speak more properly, a providential thing that the discovery of the New World was postponed to the precise period when it occurred."[13]

If America was the culmination of the progressive principle, there were other nations and races, then, that could be measured as they approached this realized ideal — or more accurately, as they advanced or retarded the progressive principle. In his histories Prescott treated three races that represented antiprogressive forces: the Moors, Jews, and Indians. As a result of their links with tradition and the past, in the case of the Jews, or their pagan beliefs, which fostered indolence and sensuality, in the Moors and Indians, these races fell before the Spaniards, who represent a vigorous and relentless force of progress.

Just as nations might be judged by their adherence to the progressive principle, so might religions. In Prescott's histories Christianity represents a marked advance over the non-Christian religions which, like the races that embrace them, are characterized by blind idolatry, indolence, sensuality, or simply a too-close adherence to the past. In Spain, Christianity was the religion of a hardy and energetic people who drove out the worshipers of antiquated or restrictive religions, the Jews and the Moors, respectively. In the New World, Spanish Christianity was one force behind the conquistadors who overthrew a pagan empire. Wherever and whenever there was the conflict between antiprogressive religions and Christianity, Prescott emphasized the inevitability of the latter's victory.

He also showed that, in consolidating the Spanish nation, the religion which had advanced the principle of progress, in turn became oppressive. As the historian of a Catholic country, he was obligated to examine the Church of Rome closely, and what he found when he came to describe the Inquisition alienated him from Catholicism. Considering Prescott's liberal Unitarianism and his religious credo arrived at after long and earnest study, this reaction is not surprising. "To do well, act justly, to fear, and to love God — and our neighbor as ourselves — in these are the essence of religion," he wrote in the *Memoranda*. "To do this is the safest, our only safe course. For what we can believe we are not responsible (supposing we examine candidly and patiently). For what we do, we shall indeed be accountable. The doctrines of the Saviour unfold the whole code of morals by which our conduct should be regulated. . . . On these then I will rest" (I, 211 - 12). Holding these beliefs and hostile to the restrictive influences of any orthodoxy, Prescott depicted the Catholic Church as the arch-antiprogressive institution.

David Levin argues that the Romantic historians were antiauthoritarian and anticlerical before they were anti-Catholic: "The central target of their criticism was authoritarianism, 'Absolutism,' 'regal and sacerdotal despotism' — not so much religious doctrine as temporal policy, including Church government."[14] Yet in Prescott's case, his language and tone suggest that Catholicism had a monopoly on absolutism. While he might criticize blind faith in orthodox Unitarianism and regard a belief in the Trinity as monstrous, he never brings the asperity to these concepts that he does to Catholicism: "The glorious Reformation gave an electric shock to the intellect, long benumbed under the influence of a tyrannical priesthood." More striking is his apology for intolerance when practiced by Protestants: "It was a blot on their characters, but one which they share in common with most reformers. . . . The martyr for conscience' sake cannot comprehend the necessity of leniency to those who denounce those truths for which he is prepared to lay down his own life. If he set so little value on his own life, is it natural he should set more on that of others?"[15]

Rationalism, Romanticism, progress, democracy, Christianity — the important influences shaping Prescott's historical point of view — are reflected in the individual histories. His concern for cause-and-effect relationships, particularly the effects of environment and geography on a people; his skepticism about mysterious accounts (usually religious) of historical happenings; his belief in a providentially directed evolution of nationalism and the eventual triumph of the progressive principle; his interest in the development of democratic institutions; his treatment of the conflict between Christian and non-Christian forces; and his criticism of the repressive and feudal quality of the Church of Rome — all of these are integral parts of his treatment of the Spanish theme.

II   *The Historian as Artist*

Working from a carefully considered theory of historical composition that required him to "display the various powers of a novelist or dramatist," Prescott approached the writing of history as a literary artist. His *Literary Memoranda* are filled with instructions for attaining unity of theme, vivid characterization, effective organization, and picturesque delineation of incident — goals essential for the novelist as well as the historian. In developing a theory of composition that would combine accurate research and literary art, Prescott drew on his extensive reading of the classical historians and the Rationalist and Romantic historians of the eighteenth and nineteenth centuries. The theory was eclectic, ideally suited, as we shall see, for treating such broad themes as Spain's rise to power and her conquests in the New World.

Of utmost importance to Prescott was the principle of thematic unity. The historian must strive, he wrote in his review of Bancroft's *United States*, to detect and skillfully keep before the reader "some great principle of action, if such exist, that may give unity and, at the same time, importance to the theme." It was a difficult task. "Few have succeeded in weaving an harmonious tissue from the motley and tangled skein of general history." The Swiss historian Sismondi had accomplished it, however, in his sixteen-volume history of the Italian Republics by keeping before the reader the principle of the rise and fall of liberty. "It is the key-note to every revolution that occurs," Prescott noted. "It gives an harmonious tone to the many-colored canvas, which would else have offended by its glaring contrasts and the startling violence of its transitions."[16] In the works of the French historian, Gabriel Bonnot de Mably, whose *Sur l'Etude de l'Histoire* Prescott read ten times, he found a unifying principle similar to Sismondi's: "I like particularly [Mably's] notion of the necessity of giving an interest as well as utility to History by letting events tend to some obvious point or moral. — In short in paying such attention to the development of events tending to this leading result as one would in the construction of a romance or drama" (*Memoranda*, I, 139). As early as 1830 Prescott was conceiving the organization of his first history in terms of Mably's theory, and acknowledging the influence.

To insure unity of theme and dramatic form, Prescott carefully organized his histories. Since he was concerned with tracing large patterns of action such as the rise of a monarchy or the fall of a civilization, he typically began with what his secretary Edmund Otis called a "grand outline" and then planned the general arrangements and proportions of his work. But since it was as necessary to provide fullness of treatment as it was to maintain reader interest, Prescott had to strike a balance between narrative passages, his obvious forte, and those passages that were expository and frequently philosophical. For this reason it was necessary in the early stages of his outlining to classify the various topics he planned to treat and to divide them into books or chapters.

In planning these divisions of the narrative and expository sections, Prescott followed the example of Voltaire who had organized his work according to a topical principle rather than a chronological order. Prescott approved of the French historian's method in his *Essai sur les Moeurs*, of devoting separate chapters to letters, religion, and manners. It enabled the reader, Prescott felt, "to arrive more expeditiously at the results, for which alone history is valuable," and it allowed the writer to "convey with more certainty and facility his own impressions."[17] Such a method, furthermore, would be particularly suitable for Prescott, who in separate expository chapters could develop his description or argument without impeding the interest of the purely narrative sections. In Prescott's opinion, both kinds of writing were necessary, but it was crucial that they be kept separate. That which was narrative and nothing else, he reminded himself in the *Literary Memoranda*, should not be interrupted by digressions or irrelevant matter.

If careful organization could insure thematic unity and dramatic form, it might also prevent anticlimax — to Prescott, a flaw no less serious in a history than in a novel. Washington Irving, he noted, had made the mistake of continuing his *Columbus* for two volumes beyond the discovery of the New World and thereby lost the reader's interest. Forewarned of the specific dangers facing the historian, Prescott was on his guard when he undertook the planning of *The Conquest of Mexico*. Knowing that Cortés' life after the final conquest had to be treated despite the danger of anticlimax, Prescott carefully gauged the length he would devote to it: "I go on with Cortés to his death. But I must take care not to make this tail piece too long, like Irving's. A hundred pages will be quite enough" (*Memoranda*, II, 68).

III   *Character*

"The *human character* is the most interesting subject of contemplation to *every* reader," Prescott noted in the *Memoranda* (I, 117). It would bear keeping in mind, since biography was an essential element in his histories. Of interest in its own right, the portrayal of character was also the major means of giving unity and dramatic form to a history. "Above all, keep character, — & especially the pervading, predominant character of the hero in view," Prescott reminded himself. "Omit no act or word of his, that can illustrate it. Interest is created out of character" (*Memoranda*, II, 70).

From Prescott's reading of the classical historians, Tacitus and Thucydides, he found early precedent for the shift of emphasis from description and events to men. Nearer his own time he discovered examples of characterization which he consciously imitated. Voltaire's *Life of Charles XII*, he found, had "all the interest of a novel." In developing the character of the hero, its author "fixes its prominent traits early on the reader's mind & loses no opportunity by personal anecdotes, remarks of the hero, or his own reflections to exhibit them in the strongest point of view possible under every change of situation" (*Memoranda*, I, 118). He was further encouraged to attempt dramatic presentation of the characters in his histories by the example of the French historian, Amable Barante, in whose *Histoire des Ducs de Bourgoyne* Prescott observed that the actors were made to speak in their own persons. The dialogue was supplied by extracts from their correspondence, public acts, and documents.

Prescott was not limited, however, to histories for the techniques of characterization. In his *History as Romantic Art*, David Levin has shown how the New England historians adopted the Romantic literary conventions of their time and thereby gave their historical figures a deeper reality than they otherwise would have had. One of the means of accomplishing this was through "portraiture," the practice of writing a sketch of a character when he first appeared, thus establishing his predominant traits early in the reader's mind. Usually based on a contemporary portrait of the subject, the sketch, Levin explains, might be used frequently to keep before the reader "a visual idea of the character's nature."[18]

Closely linked with the portrait was another Romantic convention: depiction of the central figure as "the representative man," in Levin's terms, "the incarnation of the People,"[19] one who represented their genius and embodied those national qualities peculiar to them. Moreover, in keeping with Romantic conceptions of the hero, the central figure of the history characteristically displayed a certain loftiness — a grandeur that won the admiration of the people. Coupled with this loftiness was a major emphasis on the leader's qualities of constancy and endurance — always in the face of great hardships.

These conventions — the portrait, representative quality, loft-iness, indomitable will, and endurance — are all present in Prescott's depiction of Cortés:

Cortés at this time was thirty-three, or perhaps thirty-four, years of age. In stature he was rather above the middle size. His complexion was pale; and his large dark eye gave an expression of gravity to his countenance, not to have been expected in one of his cheerful temperament. . . . His manners, frank and soldier-like, concealed a most cool and calculating spirit. With his gayest humor there mingled a settled air of resolution, which made those who approached him feel they must obey, and which infused something like awe into the attachment of his most devoted followers. Such a combination, in which love was tempered by authority, was the one probably best calculated to inspire devotion in the rough and turbulent spirits among whom his lot was to be cast.[20]

The qualities described in this portrait appear again and again at crucial times during the march to Mexico, especially in the accounts of Cortés' speeches to his troops: "The rough eloquence of the general, touching the various chords of ambition, avarice and religious zeal, sent a thrill through the bosoms of his martial audience; and receiving it with acclamations, they seemed eager to press forward under a chief who was to lead them not so much to battle, as to triumph."[21]

Later, when his men petitioned him to retreat from a dangerous position, "he was not . . . to be shaken from his purpose for a mo-ment; and, while all outward resources seemed to be fading away, and his own friends faltered or failed him, he was still true to himself." To win his men back, "he urged every argument which could touch their pride or honor as cavaliers": ancient Castilian valor, the infamy of abandoning their allies to the Aztecs, and the success of the expedition thus far. Then Cortés delivered the master stroke. If there were those who were "insensible to the motives which touch a brave man's heart," they could go. "He should feel stronger in the service of a few brave spirits than if surrounded by a host of the false or the faint-hearted." The reader has already an-ticipated the effect of the appeal: "Their blood warmed with in-dignation at the thoughts of abandoning him or the cause at such a crisis," the general's own veterans "pledged themselves to stand by him to the last."[22]

This kind of detailed examination, with emphasis on the represen-tative qualities of the central character, establishes that figure as the organizational center of the work.[23] Consequently, the narration of that character's aspirations, struggles, and triumphs — which are also those of his nation or group — develops and intensifies the thematic unity and dramatic interest of the history as a whole.

IV *Color*

Great as Prescott's emphasis on the dramatic exhibition of character was, he regarded as equally important the "picturesque delineation of incident," a result, no doubt, of his constant reading of Sir Walter Scott. The "master of the picturesque," as Prescott labeled him in a *North American Review* essay, Scott "understood better than any historian since the time of Livy how to dispose his lights and shadows so as to produce the most striking result." No man ever painted battle scenes with greater effect: "He had a natural relish for gunpowder, and his mettle roused, like that of a war-horse, at the sound of the trumpet."[24]

With his own interest in the pageantry and battles of Renaissance Spain, it is little wonder that Prescott responded so enthusiastically to the Scottish romancer. But attaining the picturesque effect could not be accomplished as easily by the historian as by the novelist. In the same essay in which he defined the picturesque quality of Scott, Prescott explained the dilemma the historian faces: "It is enough for the novelist if he be true to the spirit; the historian must be true also to the letter. He cannot coin pertinent remarks and anecdotes to illustrate the characters of his drama. . . . He must take just what Father Time has given him, just what he finds in the records of the age, setting down neither more nor less."[25]

Yet within this explanation lay the answer to the problem. It was a major fault of the modern historians, Prescott cites Barante as observing, that their works were lacking in the vivacity and freshness of the sources they used. They simply were not exploiting the old records and chronicles. Closely following the originals, according to Barante, would enable the historian "to exhibit as vivid and veracious a portraiture as possible of the times he is delineating. . . ."[26] Such was the practice of the French historian, Augustin Thierry, who, in borrowing from state papers, chronicles, and ballads, had, Prescott wrote, "succeeded in giving a series of romantic pictures, which with all the interest of romance bear on them the unquestionable stamp of reality."[27]

Picturesque details were also essential for effective character delineation, and Prescott was constantly searching for them in unpublished sources. "I have always found," he wrote Pascual de Gayangos, "a good, gossiping chronicle or memoir the best and most faithful material for the historian. . . . There is nothing so serviceable to the painter of men and manners of a distant age."[28] Official documents, Prescott again reminded Gayangos in a later letter, "furnish the cold outlines"; letters, diaries, and domestic correspondence "give us the warm coloring of history, — all that gives it its charm and interest."[29] Gayangos, who agreed, informed him that he was having four times as many letters copied as official documents.

Concerned as Prescott was with literary qualities, particularly picturesque effect, he never engaged in the impressionistic excess of Thomas Carlyle, whose *French Revolution* he severely criticized: "To attempt to color so highly what nature has already overcolored is, it appears to me, in very bad taste, and produces a grotesque and ludicrous effect, the very opposite of the sublime or beautiful."[30] But Prescott's own penchant for the stirring tale, for picturesque incident, and for vivid characters was too strong to incline him toward the more prosaic areas of history or to make him an assiduous researcher for the sake of accumulating facts for their own sake. "Nothing can be more uninteresting or more uninstructive," he recorded in the *Memoranda*, "than a tissue of facts, as in *Modern Universay History*, where the author neither gives you the sentiments, politics &c like Robertson, nor quotes the conversations &c of the actors, by going into detail like Barante, nor such natural reflections as would be suggested to every thinking writer" (I, 121). Thus he reminded himself not to go into minute details in his chapter on the Constitution of Aragon: "They will be tedious & will certainly lead me into egregious blunders." Instead he would furnish as many illustrations as he could of any principle or usage he would quote in order to give his subject general interest (*Memoranda*, I, 94 - 95).

V *Authority*

"Do not aim at *research;* there is no room for it. Only carefully ascertain the probable truth" (*Memoranda*, II, 70). It is interesting that Prescott wrote this note *after* he had completed Book I of *The Conquest of Mexico,* "View of the Aztec Civilization," which demanded painstaking study in contrast to the narrative episodes of the conquest itself. Thus we cannot be misled into thinking that he slighted his duty as a researcher. The number and extent of his notes in the histories, as well as his own comments about documentation, establish him as a conscientious scholar. In the *Memoranda* he writes of searching a whole day for a reference while Bancroft, in his history of the United States, omits references altogether and cites only the name of the authority without noting the passage (II, 63). When Prescott reviewed Bancroft's history for the *North American Review*, he commented at length on this defect, noting also the faulty format where references were placed at the side of the page rather than at the bottom, thereby making it necessary to abridge titles "at the expense of perspicuity." But it was the absence of notes that concerned him most. In a history "we want to see the grounds of his [the author's] conclusions, the scaffolding by which he has raised his structure. . . . We want to have a reason for our faith, otherwise we are merely led blindfold."

Prescott knew, however, that necessary as notes were for history, they could be detrimental to literary art. Improperly used, they often "spoil the effect of the work by drawing the attention from the continuous flow of the narrative, checking the heat that is raised by it in the reader's mind. . . ."[31]

Prescott's achievement is all the more remarkable in that he faced the difficulty squarely, constructing works that compromised neither scholarship nor the interest and drama of a splendid theme.

CHAPTER 4

Ferdinand and Isabella

BEFORE Prescott's *The History of the Reign of Ferdinand and Isabella the Catholic,* only Robertson's *History of America* and his earlier *History of Charles the Fifth* provided anything approximating partial coverage of the field of Spanish history before 1600. In foreign languages there were histories of individual subjects such as the Inquisition and the Spanish Arabs, but none had attempted to examine fifteenth-century Spain in the detail and scope that Prescott undertook in his history. He was convinced that the period of the monarchs' reign was not only the most picturesque but also the most important in Spanish history, the study of which was the proper basis for all subsequent study of Spain. As he indicated in the preface to *Ferdinand and Isabella:*

In this reign, the several States into which the country had been broken up for ages were brought under a common rule; the kingdom of Naples was conquered; America discovered and colonized; the ancient empire of the Spanish Arabs subverted; the dread tribunal of the Modern Inquisition established; the Jews, who contributed so sensibly to the wealth and civilization of the country, were banished; and, in fine, such changes introduced into the interior administration of the monarchy as have left a permanent impression on the character and condition of the nation. (VIII, xv - xvi)[1]

The passage is, in effect, the work's table of contents, for these are the topics Prescott treats as he traces his major, unifying theme which, summarized, is: the growth and development of the Spanish nation. In the process of tracing that theme, he constantly invested his work with the dramatic quality and interest he believed necessary for a history possessing literary qualities.[2]

I *Achievements*

Because achievements such as those enumerated in the preface could only be attained by a remarkable people, Prescott offers at the outset an analysis of the Spanish character. Primarily, the moral and physical energy of the Spaniard distinguished him and insured his political and military successes. These traits, Prescott shows, had been developed through long, arduous struggles with a Moorish invader and had been intensified by geography and climate. Driven into the sterile regions of northern Spain, the Spaniard could earn a "scanty subsistence" only by "a life of extreme temperance and toil," often seeking it, "sword in hand, from an enemy far superior in numbers." The result, we are told, is "a sober, hardy and independent race" that "must ultimately prevail over a nation oppressed by despotism and the effeminate indulgence to which it was naturally disposed by a sensual religion and a voluptuous climate" (VIII, 12).[3]

But if conflict with the Moors developed a spirited and warlike race, it also developed, especially among the nobility, a haughty pride, a love of independence, and an intense jealousy of their prerogatives which made them extremely sensitive to the establishment of a strong, central monarchy. Thus, having established the predominant character of the actors in his history, Prescott also accounted for the source of the divisiveness that opposed unification of the Spanish nation under one crown.

II *Unification*

Before Prescott begins the story of the struggle for monarchy, he examines the constitutions of Aragon and Castile before the fifteenth century and describes the rise to power of the commons as a result of the growth of the cities. These were not subjects that particularly appealed to him ("I must write an entertaining narrative, not an antiquarian or critical one,"[4] he wrote apropos of the Aragonese constitution), but their inclusion was essential to his history: "The course of this work will bring under review the dexterous policy by which the crown contrived to strip the aristocracy of its substantial privileges . . ." (VIII, 41). Since this frequently meant playing the commons off against the nobles, it was necessary that Prescott explain the political systems, which he does effectively and economically, furnishing illustrations of the principles he quotes, thereby giving his subject a general interest. His main interest, however, lay in the monarchs, nobles, and clerics whose intrigues and struggles for power made Spain a battlefield before unification brought order. As a result, we witness the color and cruelty of a chivalric age.

In Aragon the struggles for the succession within the royal

household provided Prescott with the elements of tragedy and melodrama which he wove into a narrative of ambition and pathos. Joan Henriquez, second wife of John II of Aragon and mother of Ferdinand, was seeking the succession for her son. She alienated the king from Carlos (his son by a previous marriage) — an act that resulted in the revolt of the people and culminated in Carlos' death by poisoning. To these events Prescott adds other episodes that characterized the age: John II's narrow escape from the mob that invaded his quarters, and the siege of Gerona, where the intrepid Joan and the ten-year-old Ferdinand, with a few followers, withstood a much larger force. But more impressive is the picture Prescott paints of a class whose desire for crowns and cities totally negated familial love or loyalty. At Carlos' death the succession of Navarre devolved on his sister Blanche, making her "tenfold an object of jealousy both to her father, the present possessor of that kingdom, and to her sister Eleanor, countess of Foix" (VIII, 150). Despite Blanche's beseeching John II not to deliver her to her enemies, she was sent to Eleanor who, after imprisoning her for two years, commanded her to be poisoned. In such a world, the protagonists of Prescott's history move. With Ferdinand's claims to the succession assured and with the climate that produced him established, Prescott turns to Castile and Isabella.

"At the date of [Isabella's] birth, her prospect of succeeding to the throne of her ancestors was even more remote than Ferdinand's prospect of inheriting that of his; and it is interesting to observe through what trials, and by what a series of remarkable events, Providence was pleased to bring about this result, and through it the union, so long deferred, of the great Spanish monarchies" (VIII, 168). With the exception of a final chapter on the Spanish Inquisition, the remainder of the first volume is devoted to this thesis. Before introducing his history's heroine, Prescott surveys the condition of Castile under the reign of Isabella's half brother Henry IV, a weak king surrounded by strong-willed counselors and a corrupt court, all of whom turned that state into a wasteland. With the currency debased, with trade, agriculture, and industry languishing, and with the authority of the monarchy and the royal courts in contempt, strong factions among the nobles developed that put Henry in jeopardy.

In a bid for a powerful ally, Henry offered the sixteen-year-old Isabella in marriage to the grand master of Calatrava, a man whose private life, Prescott tells us, "was stained with most of the licentious vices of the age." Isabella, who makes her first appearance in the history at this point, had been reared in seclusion in the little town of Arevalo, "far from the voice of flattery and falsehood." Strongly opposed to this marriage, she was saved when the intended groom died on his journey to the nuptial ceremony. Civil war followed, and with the death of a younger brother and Isabella's refusal to accept the crown, accommodation with Henry was negotiated, a major condition being Isabella's immediate recognition as heir to the crown of Castile and Leon. A faction of the royal party, however, supported Henry's daughter Joanna as heir, thus setting the stage for more civil war.

Against this background Prescott introduces Ferdinand as a possible husband for Isabella and explains the advantages that would accrue to Spain as a result of the union:

They were the descendants of one common stock, speaking one language, and living under the influence of similar institutions, which had moulded them into a common resemblance of character and manners. From their geographical position, too, they seemed destined by nature to be one nation; and, while separately they were condemned to the rank of petty and subordinate states, they might hope, when consolidated into one monarchy, to rise at once to the first class of European powers. (VIII, 203)

Furthermore, Prescott adds, Isabella was attracted to Ferdinand.

But the marriage was opposed by Henry who, with those nobles still loyal to him, was determined to prevent Ferdinand's entering Castile. With Henry's spies everywhere and his cavalry patrolling the country through which Ferdinand must travel, the first meeting between the betrothed couple was both dangerous and difficult to arrange. Traveling in disguise and with only a half-dozen attendants, Ferdinand tended the mules when they halted and served his companions at the inns. So dangerous were the times that shortly after he was presented to Isabella at Vallodolid, they were married. Prescott, not allowing the suspense to flag, concludes the chapter with the couple's requesting Henry to recognize the marriage, only to be told that "he must advise with his ministers."

When the inevitable civil war, began, Isabella actively sought the crown of Castile against the claims of Joanna. In narrating the war of the Succession, Prescott exhibits a first-rate talent for descriptive writing, providing us with precise accounts of the alignments of the opposing armies — the location of the leaders; the commanders of the center, left, and right wings; and who their opposites were across the battlefield. Thus we can follow the movements of the Duke of Alva as he turned the enemy's flank, and we can understand how the Douro River prevented their retreat. Prescott also manages to keep Ferdinand and Isabella before us — the one leading the armies and the other working at night sending dispatches and heartening the troops with her visits to the garrisons. With their victory and Ferdinand's ascension to the throne of Aragon at his father's death in 1479, the two kingdoms became "indissolubly united, and the foundations were laid of the magnificent empire which was destined to overshadow every other European monarchy" (VIII, 283).

Prescott concludes the story of unification with a detailed account of the reforms made by the young monarchs in the administration of Castile. Under separate headings he examines topics ranging from the suppression of the nobles to the efficient administration of justice, keeping Ferdinand and particularly Isabella before us, making the reforms their personal accomplishments. As a result, he establishes Isabella as both an energetic and a prudent sovereign, one who "endeavored to bind together the disjointed fragments of the state, to assign to each of its great divisions its constitutional limits, and, by depressing the aristocracy to its proper level and elevating the commons, to consolidate the whole under the lawful supremacy of the crown" (VIII, 336). With these objects accomplished, he concludes that Spain could turn to the "glorious career of discovery and conquest which it was destined to run during the remainder of the century" (VIII, 336).

III *Holy War*

The first episode in that glorious career was the conquest of Granada, the last stronghold of the Moors on the Spanish peninsula. In creating the effect of a grand design in his history, Prescott devotes an introductory chapter to the character of the Spanish Arabs and the high civilization they had achieved, suggesting in his account the inevitability of their defeat by the more progressive and vigorous Spaniards: "The lawless, predatory habits, which no discipline could effectually control in an Arab, made them ever ready for revolt" (IX, 22). Consequently, the internal wars within the Moslem states prevented their resisting the Christian forces that descended on them from the north. Thus by the middle of the thirteenth century only Granada remained in the Moors' hands: "Yet on this comparatively small point of their ancient domain the Saracens erected a new kingdom, of sufficient strength to resist, for more than two centuries, the united forces of the Spanish monarchies" (IX, 23). Defeat of the Moor is the challenge Prescott presents the new monarchs. His narration of their response to it is both more colorful and more direct than the story of unification. There is but one goal, hence one subject — the defeat of the Spanish Arabs by the capture of their capital city, Granada.

Again the king and queen play prominent roles in the story. Ferdinand distinguishes himself as a soldier and leader, while Isabella emerges as a skillful director of logistics, levying armies and navies, establishing field hospitals, and supervising the construction of roads. Their presence and contributions are constantly established in the anecdotes Prescott includes throughout his account of the war. To stop a rout, Ferdinand charges from his tent not fully armored and narrowly escapes death or capture. To his men who later remonstrate with him, he replies that "he could not stop to calculate chances when his subjects were perilling their lives for his sake" (IX, 162). No less colorful is his queen, "who, as she rode through the ranks mounted on her war-horse and clad in complete mail, afforded no bad personification of the genius of chivalry" (IX, 135). In anecdotes such as these Prescott never lets us forget that this was a chivalric age whose values were honored by both races. A Moorish knight, when asked why he spared the Spanish children who had wandered from their camp, replies: "Because I saw no beard upon their chins" (IX, 178).

The narration of battles interested Prescott more, however, and the Spanish march against Granada provided him the opportunity to exercise his talents for description. Paradoxically, his most striking account in this story of Spanish conquest is the rout of the Spanish force in the Axarquia, the chain of mountains traversing the Spaniards' line of march to Malaga. In the winding defiles of the mountains, with no room for their cavalry to maneuver, the Spanish are ambushed and thrown into disorder by the Moorish forces commanding the peaks. A sure target for the Moors who rain artillery-fire and large fragments of rock down upon them, the Spaniards face certain annihilation unless they act: ". . . at length, after having seen their best and bravest followers fall thick around them, they determined at all hazards to force a passage across the sierra in the face of the enemy. 'Better lose our lives,' said the grand master of St. James, addressing his men, 'in cutting a way through the foe, than be butchered without resistance, like cattle in the shambles' " (IX, 103).

Their response and its consequences provide Prescott with the material for some of the most vivid writing in the entire history: "At every step [of their difficult ascent] the loosened earth gave way under the pressure of the foot; and, the infantry endeavoring to support themselves by clinging to the tails and manes of the horses, the jaded animals, borne down with the weight, rolled headlong with their riders on the ranks below, or were precipitated down the sides of the numerous ravines" (IX, 104). The next morning the survivors begin their descent into an opposite valley commanded at every point by the enemy. They are a striking contrast to the "magnificent array" that began the expedition: ". . . their ranks thinned, their bright arms defaced and broken, their banners rent in pieces, or lost, . . . their countenances aghast with terror, fatigue, and famine! Despair was now in every eye; all subordination was at an end" (IX, 105). Some escaped, but "there was scarcely a family in the south but had to mourn the loss of some one of its members by death or captivity" (IX, 108).

With the exception of the account of the rout in the Axarquia, the war of Granada is primarily a story of sieges in which the cities fell one after another after being attacked and starved by the Spanish forces. The pattern is the same for each siege: besiegement, sorties from the gates, the appearance of Isabella to hearten the troops, negotiations between the Spaniards and the Moors, the opening of the gates, the purification of the town from the numerous dead bodies, the release of the Christian captives from the Moorish dungeons, where some had lingered ten or fifteen years, the consecration of the principal mosque, the distribution of crosses and bells, the entrance of the monarchs into the city and their attendance at mass, where "the glorious anthem of the Te Deum rose for the first time within its ancient walls" (IX, 184).

Consequently, the siege and surrender of Granada itself seems repetitious and anticlimactic:

In a short time, the large silver cross, borne by Ferdinand throughout the crusade, was seen sparkling in the sunbeams, while the standards of Castile and St. Jago waved triumphantly from the red towers of the Alhambra. At this glorious spectacle the choir of the royal chapel broke forth into the solemn anthem of the Te Deum, and the whole army, pentrated with deep emotion, prostrated themselves on their knees in adoration of the Lord of Hosts. (IX, 246)

In a discussion of realism in one of his interviews, William Dean Howells remarked that life is not afraid of anticlimaxes; they occur frequently. The historian cannot afford to be afraid of them either, for they are often a part of the account he must write. Fortunately Prescott was able to maintain his reader's interest in the war of Granada despite the predictable pattern and outcome of its sieges, by including the kind of information that gives military history its special appeal. His explanation of tactics, his inclusion of relevant facts and statistics (the first use of the gunpowder mine, the size of cannonballs), and his selection of anecdotes to illustrate the character of the figures and their age — all contribute to the impression of a solid and carefully researched account.

IV *Discovery*

Prescott's account of the discovery of the New World, the history's third major event, is the least satisfactory in terms of narrative treatment. Having formally acknowledged in the history's introduction that Irving's history of Columbus had stripped his own account of the discovery of the charm of novelty, Prescott apparently felt that Irving's work had obviated any necessity for him to bring his own artistry into play in telling the Columbus story. Twice in the account he alludes to the reader's previous knowledge of Columbus's history; the assumption is that he has learned it from Irving. Of the account of the voyage itself, we are informed only that "on the morning of the 3d of August, 1492, the intrepid navigator, bidding adieu to the old world, launched forth on that unfathomed waste of waters where no sail had been ever spread before" (IX, 282). Then, following some thirty-three pages describing the explusion of the Jews from Spain, we read that "the great navigator had succeeded, as is well known, after a voyage the natural difficulties of which had been much augmented by the distrust and mutinous spirits of his followers, in descrying land on Friday, the 12th of October, 1492" (IX, 315). The next sentence states that Columbus embarked in the month of January, 1493, for Spain. This was Prescott's treatment of the discovery of the New World.

The interest, therefore, lies in those expository sections where Prescott examines a wide range of topics: the effect an Italian monoploy on trade with the East had on Spanish and Portuguese explorations, Columbus's hypothesis of land to the West and his difficulty in gaining support, the immediate results of the discovery (materially they were less than was anticipated and expenses for a while exceeded the profits), the enslavement and exploitation of the Indians, and the Spanish colonial policy in general. Finally, as is typical of Prescott, he interprets the significance of the events he has examined:

Whatever be the amount of physical good or evil immediately resulting to
Spain from her new discoveries, their moral consequences were inestimable.
The ancient limits of human thought and action were overleaped; the veil
which had covered the secrets of the deep for so many centuries was
removed; another hemisphere was thrown open; and a boundless expansion
promised to science, from the infinite varieties in which nature was exhibited in those unexplored regions. (X, 260 - 61)

V *Foreign Wars*

In his account of the Italian Wars, Precott returns to writing about
the subject he enjoyed most. This time since his subject's novelty is
unimpaired by an earlier treatment, he describes in detail the ordnance, tactics, and battles, as well as the leaders and encounters
between individual knights. Having first explained the causes of the
war between the Spanish and the French in Italy, Prescott again
differentiates among the combatants on the basis of their moral and
physical energy. Relying on mercenaries and studying the science of
defense almost exclusively, "the Italian, made effeminate, if not
timid, was incapable of encountering the adventurous daring and
severe discipline of the [French] warrior" (X, 30).[5]

Against the *furia Francese* the Spaniards posed "stern resolve
[and] calm, unflinching endurance" (X, 310). In scene after scene,
Prescott shows the Spanish commander relying confidently on the
thorough discipline and "steady nerve" of his infantry. It is on the
knights and leaders; however, that Prescott concentrates in this war.
Just as Isabella was the "soul" of the Granadine war, Gonsalvo de
Cordova, leader of the Spanish forces, is the genius of the Italian
Wars. Bold, innovative, cautious when necessary, proud yet
generous, and perceptive of the qualities of the Spanish soldier, he is
a memorable figure. It is his kind who participate in the jousts and
tournaments staged throughout the wars; in them we discern "the
last gleams of the light of chivalry, which illuminated the darkness of
the Middle Ages" (X, 315). Pageantry and courtesy, however, were,
as Prescott makes clear, the prerogatives of class. While prisoners of
rank were well treated, the soldier or peasant was "abandoned
without remorse to all the caprices and cruelties of military license"
(X, 325 - 26).

The detailed and precise descriptions Prescott gives to ordnance
and tactics indicate that these subjects interested him as much as did
military leaders, usually the heroes of his histories. The Italians, for
example, are "panic-struck at the aspect of [French] troops so

different from their own, and so superior to them in organization, science, and military equipment" (X, 28). We understand why when Prescott contrasts their artillery: the Italian field pieces (which discharge stone balls) are small copper tubes covered with wood and hides and mounted on unwieldly carriages drawn by oxen. The lightly mounted, bronze French cannon fire iron balls and are horse drawn. While the French fire is rapid, accurate, and destructive, the Italian guns are "worked so awkwardly that the besieged . . . had time between the discharges to repair the mischief inflicted by them" (X, 32).

Typical of the military portions of the history are such detailed explanations of tactics as the following account of the Swiss pike:

The Swiss were formed into battalions varying from three to eight thousand men each. They wore little defensive armor, and their principal weapon was the pike, eighteen feet long. Formed into these solid battalions, which, bristling with spears all around, received the technical appellation of the *hedgehog*, they presented an invulnerable front on every quarter. In the level field, with free scope allowed for action, they bore down all opposition, and received unshaken the most desperate charges of the steel-clad cavalry on their terrible array of pikes. They were too unwieldy, however, for rapid or complicated manoeuvres; they were easily disconcerted by any unforeseen impediment, or irregularity of the ground; and the event proved that the Spanish foot, armed with its short swords and bucklers, by breaking in under the long pikes of its enemy, could succeed in bringing him to close action, where his formidable weapon was of no avail. It was repeating the ancient lesson of the Roman legion and the Macedonian phalanx. (X, 31)

The Spanish cavalry profits from more recent lessons learned in the war of Granada. After a brief skirmish near Barleta with a French rear guard, the Spanish cavalry retreats with the enemy in pursuit. Suddenly the pursuers find themselves attacked on the flank by the Spanish infantry which has just arrived on the scene. Their disorder becomes complete when "the flying cavalry of the Spaniards, suddenly wheeling round in the rapid style of the Moorish tactics, charged them boldly in front" (X, 320). This is the stuff of the history, and Prescott works it in whenever possible.

Despite the numerous battles described in the volume, Prescott makes each one vivid and distinct, frequently by introducing an anecdote. When a spark explodes the Spanish powder magazine, Gonsalvo steadies his men, calling "Courage, soldiers! these are the beacon-lights of victory! We have no need of our guns at close

quarters" (X, 343). In another battle a Spanish standard-bearer, his
right hand shot away, refuses to relinquish the banner because, as he
insists, he has "one hand still left." Given such men as these, victory
was inevitable, and its consequences, Prescott explains, were far-
reaching. Ferdinand, who had had charge of the war, had gained
recognition as the defender of the faith and a reputation for sagacity
and prudence; important innovations in military science had taken
place; Spain was now a world power. No longer cooped up on the
peninsula, she had learned her strength in "collision with other
powers on a common scene of action" (X, 92).

VI *Dark Pages*

In recording the glorious achievements of the reign of Ferdinand
and Isabella, Prescott constantly revealed his sympathy with the
Spaniards whenever their accomplishments were in harmony with
progress and principle. But there were episodes in which it was impossible for the historian to maintain either his enthusiasm for the
Spaniards or his objectivity in recording their transgressions. To
describe the Spanish Inquisition, the expulsion of the Jews and
Moors from Spain, and the exploitation and enslavement of the Indian in the New World necessitated a shift in his point of view. In
relating these dark pages in Spain's history, Prescott wrote as a
nineteenth-century Protestant, committed to progress and reason,
who must record and judge the excesses of religious fanaticism and
the destructive effects of greed.

At the beginning of his account of the modern Inquisition, "one of
the grossest abuses that ever disgraced humanity," Prescott establishes his point of view: "In the present liberal state of
knowledge, we look with disgust at the pretentions of any human being, however exalted, to invade the sacred rights of conscience, in-
alienably possessed by every man" (VIII, 337). Prescott then traces
the Inquisition in Spain from its introduction in Aragon in 1242 to its
organization in Castile in the reign of Isabella, where the Spanish
Jews became its victims. In the course of this history we meet the
Inquisitor-General, Thomas de Torquemada: "This man, who concealed more pride under his monastic weeds than might have furnished forth a convent of his order, was one of that class with whom
zeal passes for religion, and who testify their zeal by a fiery persecution of those whose creed differs from their own" (VIII, 355).

The account of the Inquisition is vivid, terrifying, and
documented. The absurd tests to determine heresy (did the accused

wear cleaner clothes on the Jewish Sabbath than on other days, sit at a table with Jews, turn his face to the wall when dying, etc.?); the stone scaffold in Seville with statues of the four prophets attached to the corners to which the condemned were tied and burned; the procedure of the Inquisitional courts — these are the elements in this history of fanaticism. We follow an accused heretic from his arrest, incarceration, and torture in the secret chambers of the Inquisition to his participation in an *auto da fe* (act of faith). This last, Prescott writes, was "the most imposing spectacle, probably, which has been witnessed since the ancient Roman triumph, and which . . . was intended, somewhat profanely, to represent the terrors of the Day of Judgment" (VIII, 368). Its climax came when the condemned prisoner, clad in a coarse woolen garment "well garnished with figures of devils and flames of fire, . . . typical of the heretic's destiny hereafter," was led to the stake. He was one of the 8,800 "impenitent heretics" burned during the eighteen years of Torquemada's ministry (VIII, 370).

On March 30, 1492 an edict signed at Granada called for the exile of all unbaptized Jews regardless of age, sex, or condition. This edict was followed ten years later by another one which exiled all the unbaptized Moors from the kingdoms of Castile and Leon, the consequences of which led Prescott to exercise his privilege of commentary: "Castile might now boast, for the first time in eight centuries, that every outward stain, at least, of infidelity was purified from its bosom"; but it was accomplished, the historian adds, "by the most detestable expedients which sophistry could devise and oppression execute" (X, 204).

The pattern of oppression that frequently accompanied the magnificent achievements of the monarchs continued into the New World. Within thirty-eight years of the discovery, more than twelve million Indians were wantonly destroyed. Most of them were killed as a result of the enforced labor necessary to extract the wealth of the New World. In part, Prescott attributes this ill treatment to the nature of the colonists, many of whom were convicts. He records also that "it was the received opinion among good Catholics of that period, that heathen and barbarous nations were placed by the circumstances of their infidelity without the pale both of spiritual and civil rights" (X, 225).

For Prescott the dark pages in Spanish history were the result of the unlimited power of the Catholic Church, an institution he regarded as medieval and sinister. Its priesthood in particular he held suspect because of its influence over the people through the confession. As is apparent from Prescott's commentary on the Inquisition and the enslavement of the Indian, he lost no opportunity to denounce the Church when it was oppressive, but he recognized that there were also good men in the Church. To the fanatical Torquemada, he could oppose Fray Fernando de Talavera, archbishop of Granada, a pious man who learned Arabic so that he could attract the Moors to his church. He respected Bartolomé de Las Casas (the inspector of Indian affairs) who labored so long to protect the Indian. But Prescott was forced to admit that such men were exceptions.

He was never ambivalent in his treatment of the Church, though. If he was not morally indignant at its cruelty and oppression, he was amused at its innumerable accounts of miracles, all documented. The latter he repeats verbatim in the text or comments on in a facetious footnote. The sun standing still in the sky for four hours to allow a Spanish victory at Oran prompts him to wonder in a footnote why so astonishing a miracle should escape the notice of all Europe. He concludes that "this universal silence may be thought, indeed, the greater miracle of the two" (XI, 156).

VII *Protagonists*

In Isabella of Castile, Prescott found the perfect heroine for his history, one who would give unity to the work as she and the Spanish nation together grew to greatness. She becomes the representative character, that person who embodies the genius of the people. In particular, it is her moral virtues, her chaste and sober character, that Prescott emphasizes. Born in 1451 at Madrigal and reared in seclusion at Arevalo, she did not forget her "lessons of practical piety" or "her deep reverence for religion" when summoned to the royal palace with its "scenes of levity and licentiousness." Such virtue had practical political consequences for Isabella, in that her sedate conduct and the decorum of her court, so strongly in contrast to that of her half-brother Henry IV's, attracted allies to her cause in the war of the Succession.

Sedate conduct, however, does not inspire impressive narrative. Prescott was fortunate in having a heroine who could display a more aggressive side of her character. Forced by the war of the Succession to make the sudden transformation from girl to queen, Isabella becomes in Prescott's treatment a formidable antagonist. Working at night sending dispatches, traveling by horseback while pregnant to visit garrisons and confirm their allegiance, she raised a loyal army. In the process she became regal. Her succession confirmed, she appears in subsequent scenes as forceful, direct, and increasingly aware of the duties of queenship and the homage due it. When the townspeople seized Segovia, she faced them down alone, informing them that "she was queen of Castile; that the city was hers, moreover, by right of inheritance; and that she was not used to receive conditions from rebellious subjects" (VIII, 291).

Nor was rank a mitigating influence when her authority was challenged. When the son of the powerful admiral of Castile violated the safe conduct she had given a young nobleman, she had him imprisoned and exiled. Her more typical role, however, was inspiring loyalty and confidence in her subjects by her devoted service to the nation. Presiding with Ferdinand at least once a week in the tribunals, she inspired one observer to write: "This was indeed the golden age of justice" (VIII, 302). She consolidated her position further by her active participation in the war of Granada, where, in addition to raising men and artillery and establishing field hospitals, she was an important source of morale — in Prescott's words, "the soul of this war."

Whether as animating spirit of the Granadine war, civil administrator, sponsor of Columbus, devout Catholic, loyal wife, or loving mother, Isabella is for Prescott the nonpareil. Consequently we read in vain the pages of *Ferdinand and Isabella* for one word of adverse critism of the Spanish queen by the author. While there are numerous examples of her lofty sentiments and deeds that would do credit to one of her knights, the picture of Isabella never quite comes into focus; it is too idealized. If Prescott could not reconcile to our satisfaction the lone young woman who cowed the mob in the street at Segovia with the older, assiduous embroiderer of altar pieces, we excuse the failure as one of technique. A more serious flaw is his inability to explain satisfactorily how Isabella could, on one hand, beat down every attempt of the Church to encroach on the royal prerogative, and on the other, allow the Inquisition into Spain.

What especially troubles us is the special pleading Prescott engages in to exonerate his heroine:

With regard to Isabella, moreover, it must be borne constantly in mind, as has been repeatedly remarked in the course of this history, that she had been used to surrender her own judgment in matters of conscience to those spiritual guardians who were supposed in that age to be its rightful depositaries, and the only casuists who could safely determine the doubtful line of duty. Isabella's pious disposition, and her trembling solicitude to discharge her duty at whatever cost of personal inclination, greatly enforced the precepts of education. In this way, her very virtues became the source of her errors. (IX, 307 - 308)[6]

However flawed his portrayal of Isabella, Prescott keeps her in the forefront on his narrative as much as possible and makes her a unifying force in the history. He demonstrates without qualification her role in Spain's rise and underlines her role as the soul of the nation by revealing the dissolution of order and loss of grandeur in Castile following her death.

While unstinting in his admiration for Isabella, Prescott finds it difficult to be objective about Ferdinand. From the outset he establishes a head-and-heart dichotomy in the Spanish monarchs and maintains constantly the queen's natural, sensitive qualities in contrast to Ferdinand's cold logic. Both monarchs, he observes, "exhibited a practical wisdom in their own personal relations, . . . which, however it may have savored of worldly policy in Ferdinand, was, in his consort, founded on the purest and most exalted principle" (VIII, 334). But in documenting the beneficial results to Spain of Ferdinand's craft and intrigue, Prescott inadvertently makes the king the more interesting figure. He had no problem in reconciling disparate qualities in Ferdinand's character. From his first appearance he is forceful and decisive. Completely his own man, though not yet twenty, he informed the archbishop of Toledo, Isabella's staunchest supporter in the war of the Succession, that "he was not to be put in leading-strings, like so many of the sovereigns of Castile" (VIII, 223). He challenged Alphonso of Portugal to settle by personal combat the latter's claim to the succession of Castile, and he distinguished himself both as warrior and as commander in chief in the war of Granada.

It is Ferdinand's political role, however, that interests Prescott most. He recognizes the monarch's foresight in being the first to introduce resident embassies in foreign nations, and he approves his policy of quickly meeting the Moorish overtures to surrender their cities. Prescott is also impressed by Ferdinand's use of the old Aragonese claims to Naples as a basis for Spanish involvement in the Italian Wars, wars which he skillfully managed and which established Spain as a European power.

The greatest test of Ferdinand's political skill, Prescott shows, came at home with the death of Isabella, when the crown of Castile passed to his daughter Joanna and her Austrian consort Philip. Subject to fits of melancholy and insanely jealous of her handsome and "dissipated" husband, Joanna was losing her mind, a fact well known to the Spanish *cortes*. Urged by his counselors to reassume the title of King of Castile, Ferdinand refused, recognizing that the attempt would mean war and that victory "must bring unspeakable calamity on the country." Instead he waited for Philip to attempt to rule Castile, an act that would alienate the Castilian nobility. In the meantime he detached the French from the interest of Philip by marrying Germaine, one of the sisters of Louis XII. Though Prescott never forgives him for marrying one so inferior to Isabella, he recognizes the policy behind the act. Philip died in 1506, and Ferdinand returned to Castile in 1507 to act as administrator for his daughter and as guardian for her son.

In Ferdinand's adroit and successful playing of the game of policy, he becomes for Prescott "the representative of the peculiar genius of the age," a conclusion Prescott supports with a quotation from Machiavelli: "Nothing gains estimation for a prince like great enterprises. Our own age has furnished a splendid example of this in Ferdinand of Aragon. We may call him a new king, since from a feeble one he has made himself the most renowned and glorious monarch of Christendom . . ." (XI, 255). In contrasting the Spanish king and queen, Prescott writes: "Isabella, discarding all the petty artifices of state policy, and pursuing the noblest ends by the noblest means, stands far above her age" (XI, 252). He has shown, however, that diverse as their conceptions of statecraft were, together they presided over a nation whose grandeur had never been equaled on the Spanish peninsula.

A host of other memorable figures appear in *Ferdinand and Isabella*, each revealed in an anecdote illustrating his character and evaluated in an obituary assessing his contribution to his age: the ascetic Cardinal Ximenes; the mad Joanna of Castile; the voluptuary Charles VIII of France; the crafty John of Aragon; Columbus; and the author's favorite, Gonsalvo de Cordova, "The Great Captain." We see Torquemada when he learns that the Jews had sent a negotiator with thirty thousand ducats to influence Ferdinand and Isabella not to sign the proclamation banishing them. He bursts into the monarchs' chamber holding a crucifix before him, crying: "Judas Iscariot sold his master for thirty pieces of silver. Your Highnesses would sell him anew for thirty thousand; here he is, take him, and barter him away" (IX, 290). Torquemada hurls the crucifix on the table and flees the room.

Strong egos and the pride and pageantry of a chivalric age furnished Prescott with the scenes and set speeches for a colorful, dramatic narrative. To his credit as an imaginative author and skillful researcher, though, he exploited the old chronicles and diaries for what they reveal about that age.

VIII *Persona*

Because Prescott in his authorial commentary consistently expresses a Protestant, progressive, and ethical point of view, he himself becomes as distinct and impressive as any of the figures who move across the pages of *Ferdinand and Isabella*. We encounter a strong personality that philosophizes and renders judgments freely. Whether determining which monarch, a weak or a wicked one, causes more mischief to the realm or who is more dangerous, an atheist or a religious fanatic, Prescott makes his philosophical position clear: " . . . fanaticism is so far subversive of the most established principles of morality, that under the dangerous maxim, 'For the advancement of the faith, all means are lawful,' . . . it not only excuses but enjoins the commission of the most revolting crimes, as a sacred duty" (VIII, 376).

Of the partitioning of Naples by Ferdinand and Louis XII, Prescott comments: "Similar instances of political robbery (to call it by the coarse name it merits) have occurred in later times; but never one founded on more flimsy pretexts, or veiled under a more detestable mask of hypocrisy" (X, 279). More revealing of his point of view is his reaction to Gonsalvo's breach of faith to the Duke of Calabria, whom he had promised freedom when the duke surrendered Tarento. Informed later that Ferdinand wanted the duke imprisoned, Gonsalvo took the opinion of "certain learned jurists" who found his oath not binding since a general's first obligation was to his master who, in turn, was not bound by an oath made without his specific sanction. Prescott's comment is that "the man who trusts his honor to the tampering of casuists has parted with it already" (X, 298). We recognize, then, a persona whose moral stance and impatience with weakness and guile preclude ambiguous attitudes or muted prejudices.

Frequently Prescott speaks directly to his reader as he explicitly comments on the organization of his history: "I have deferred to the present chapter a consideration of the important changes introduced into the interior administration of Castile, after the accession of

Isabella, in order to present a connected and comprehensive view of them to the reader without interrupting the progress of the military narrative" (VIII, 284). Such planning on Prescott's part was necessary, considering the topical organization of the history. Influenced by Voltaire, as we have seen, Prescott does not limit himself to a strict chronological narrative, but instead treats in separate chapters the military, political, religious, and cultural history of the Spanish nation. Therefore his reader alternately reads narrative accounts of campaigns and inquisitional proceedings and expository chapters on the Spanish Arab culture and Spanish colonial policy.

If the history were to be coherent and the vast amount of material made significant, Prescott had to use such rhetorical devices as numbering and recapitulation to give emphasis to his material. Since literary craftsmanship was so important to him, he had to advance the history economically by briefly summarizing events and leading his reader to the more significant ones. Typical are such transitional sections as: "Notwithstanding the importance of the results in the war of Granada, a detail of the successive steps by which they were achieved would be most tedious and trifling. . . . Without pursuing the chronological order of events, it is probable that the end of history will be best attained by presenting a concise view of the general policy pursued by the sovereigns in the conduct of the war" (IX, 119).

At other times he justifies his inclusion of material by informing us of its significance in advance: "As it was that [the reign of John II], however, which gave birth to Isabella, the illustrious subject of our narrative, it will be necessary to pass its principal features under review, in order to obtain a correct idea of her government" (VIII, 110). To increase his reader's retention of the significant points of his history, he lists the results of a reign, a campaign, or the characteristics of a culture; the reasons for the military success of the Spanish Arabs, the effects of the Italian Wars, the meaning of the conquest of Granada, the six important reforms in the internal administration of Castile, thus giving us not only the pageantry and sweep of epic struggles but the equally interesting explanation of their consequences, both immediate and long range.

IX *Authority*

Ferdinand and Isabella has the ring of authority that is achieved, in part, by the sheer abundance of its factual information — the annual gold yield of Hispaniola, the cost of the campaign against Louis

XII, the size of the cannonballs in a siege, the first use of the gunpowder mine, the number of Jews expelled from Castile. These are the facts that shore up the more colorful passages of the history and win our confidence in the author as a researcher. There are also the materials Prescott had diligently collected, of which he was justifiably proud: "I flatter myself that I have been enabled to secure whatever can materially conduce to the illustration of the period in question, whether in form of chronicle, memoir, private correspondence, legal codes, or official documents" (VIII, xviii). He is equally diligent in the preparation of the notes for the history, in some instances consuming as much time in their preparation as in writing the text. In them he may explain the Arab conception of military service or he may balance one authority against another concerning a conflicting interpretation.[7]

Of particular benefit to future historians were the bibliographical essays that appeared throughout the history, in which Prescott identifies the previous workers in the field and discusses their merits and defects. Francisco Martínez Marina's valuable work on the *cortes* of Castile, for example, provides "a full exposition of the appropriate functions assigned to the several departments of government, and with the parliamentary history of Castile deduced from original, unpublished records. It is unfortunate that his copious illustrations are arranged in so unskillful a manner as to give a dry and repulsive air to the whole work" (VIII, 60). To these facts, notes, and bibliographical essays must be added those expository sections, already discussed, in which Prescott explains the causes and consequences of decisions and events. Taken together, these elements provide the substratum for a remarkable history of an illustrious reign.

CHAPTER 5

"An Epic in Prose"

F OUR months after the publication of *The History of the Reign of Ferdinand and Isabella the Catholic*, three letters, all written on the noctograph and dated April 21, 1838, were sent to Thomas Gonzales, Arthur Middleton, and Martín de Navarrete. These men were, respectively, the keeper of the archives at Simancas, the secretary of the United States legation at Madrid, and the president of the Royal Academy in Madrid and compiler and editor of the records of the Spanish maritime discoveries in America. The contents of the three letters were similar: each alluded to a copy of *Ferdinand and Isabella* that the author had sent to the recipient; each requested assistance in securing materials for a forthcoming project; each offered an explanation of the author's reasons for undertaking that project. A paragraph from the letter to Navarrete is illustrative:

My history of the Catholic Kings has met with so favorable a reception from my countrymen that I feel stimulated to pursue the subject of Spanish history further, and no portion of it has greater interest for us than that connected with our own country, and which in itself is singularly romantic, like the Conquest of Mexico and Peru. The story has been often told however, and it would not be worth while to attempt it anew without the use of such original documents as will give it the highest authenticity.[1]

In other letters and in the *Literary Memoranda*, Prescott emphasized repeatedly the attraction of the subject for readers and the necessity for new and original documents. There were earlier works treating the conquest of Mexico, in both Spanish and English. Bernal Diaz's eyewitness account of the conquest, which Prescott had used extensively, had been translated, as had the *Historia de la Conquista de México* of Antonio de Solís and the *Storia Antica del Messico* of F. X. Clavigero. Robertson's account of the conquest appeared in his *History of America* (1777), but as Prescott pointed out, it was only an outline. Furthermore, "a deficiency of authentic materials" had prevented the Scottish historian from giving "a minute or a very faithful view of the Mexican civilization."[2]

Hence there was a need, not only for an accurate history of the conquest, but for a history of the ancient Mexican civilization and for a subsequent biography of Cortés, neither of which had been examined before. To write this kind of history Prescott needed the original documents his friends were acquiring for him in England, Mexico, and on the Continent. By the time of the history's completion in 1843,[3] he could write Colonel Aspinwall, his agent in England, that he had acquired, in addition to

all the printed works of any value, . . . ample materials from the Archives of the Royal Academy of History of Madrid: They consist of the correspondence and diaries of the Conquerors, dispatches of the Court, instructions, official documents of every description, forming a mass of more than five thousand folio pages of manuscript, and making the most authentic basis for a history of the Conquest, and one to which previous historians native or foreign have not had access.[4]

The complimentary copies of *Ferdinand and Isabella* had brought an ample return.

Confident of the interest the subject would have for readers and assured by the collection of unpublished manuscripts in his library that his history would be authentic, Prescott began composition in October 1839. There were interruptions and brief journeys, as well as long periods of inactivity, but his eye served him better during the writing of *Mexico* than at any other time in his career. When he worked, he made good progress, sometimes writing twelve pages a day. The one threat to the success of the project was removed when Washington Irving in the winter of 1838 abandoned his plan to write the story of the conquest when he learned that Prescott had begun work on the subject.[5]

I *Conception*

It is not difficult to understand why Irving's imagination had been fired by the conquest when we read Prescott's conception of it in the *Literary Memoranda* for July 1839: "The narrative is a beautiful epic. It has all the interest which daring, chivalrous enterprise, stupendous achievements, worthy of an age of knight-errantry, a magical country, the splendors of a rich barbaric court, and extraordinary personal qualities in the hero . . . can give." A few pages later he concluded: "In short, the true way of conceiving the subject is, not as a philosophical theme, but as an *epic in prose. . . .*" (*Memoranda*, II, 29, 32)

It was a brilliant conception, but inherent in it were problems of form. If Prescott was to narrate the conquest of an ancient civilization, it would be necessary to describe that civilization in detail, not only to provide information about an area hitherto shrouded in ignorance or which had been the subject of fantastic speculation,[6] but also to give its full significance and establish its formidability to the handful of adventurers who undertook its conquest. Furthermore, having followed step by step the epic's protagonist from Hispaniola into the City of Mexico, it would be unthinkable not to trace his subsequent career. Thus it was necessary for Prescott to divide the history into three parts: a lengthy introduction to the Aztec civilization, the conquest itself, and Cortés' subsequent career. Fully aware that the first part could detract from the unity of the work, while the last might be anticlimactic, Prescott held to this structure. The result is a truly organic work in which the history of an ancient civilization is carefully and honestly presented before an accurate and exciting narration of the conquest itself, which concludes logically with an account of the conqueror's later life.[7]

II   *The Aztec Civilization*

Prescott's description of the Aztec civilization proved the most difficult part of the history to write. Originally planned as a hundred-page introduction, it grew to 250 and occupied Prescott for two and a half years. In preparing it he drew on recent research in Mexican geography and civilization, the manuscript collections of Lord Kingsborough and Henri Ternaux-Compans; the older authorities Antonio de Herrera, Juan de Torquemada, and Bernardino de Sahagun; and the manuscript accounts of Fernando de Alva Ixtlilxochitl, Toribio de Benavente, and Diego Muñoz Camargo. The result of his diligence, skillful editing, and assessments of conflicting accounts and anthropological speculations is an authoritative and vivid history of the Aztec civilization.

Organized by topics, the six-chapter introduction examines climate, geography, primitive races (Chapter I); Aztec nobility, laws, military institutions (II); Mexican mythology, priesthood, human sacrifices (III); hieroglyphics, chronology, agriculture, mechanical arts, domestic manners (IV and V). The sixth chapter is a narrative history of the golden age of a neighboring people, the Tezcuzans.[8] For his descriptions of geography and climate Prescott relied on the accounts of recent travelers in Mexico, particularly those of his friend Fanny Calderón de la Barca, whose descriptions he incorporated into his text. The *tierra caliente*, the malaria region, the volcanic scenery, the cordilleran range, and the Valley of Mexico are all described, as is the effect of the climate changes on the traveler: "His limbs recover their elasticity, he breathes more freely."

In the second chapter Prescott establishes the martial instincts of the Aztecs, thereby preparing us for the ferocity of the encounters between them and the Spaniards:

But the great aim of the Aztec institutions, to which private discipline and public honors were alike directed, was the profession of arms. In Mexico, as in Egypt, the soldier shared with the priest the highest consideration. The king, as we have seen, must be an experienced warrior. The tutelary deity of the Aztecs was the god of war. A great object of their military expeditions was to gather hecatombs of captives for his altars. . . . Every war, therefore, became a crusade; and the warrior, animated by a religious enthusiasm like that of the early Saracen or the Christian crusader, was not only raised to a contempt of danger, but courted it, for the imperishable crown of martyrdom. (I, 56) [9]

The third chapter, a detailed and chilling account of human sacrifices, justifies the conquest as a providential means of terminating an abominable practice. After commenting on the plurality of Aztec deities (there were thirteen principal gods and over two hundred inferior ones), Prescott describes two who figure prominently in the story of the conquest. Huitzilopochtli, the Mexican war god and patron deity of the nation, is a "sanguinary monster" whose "altars reeked with the blood of human hecatombs in every city of the empire" (I, 70). The other, Quetzalcoatl, god of air, had been the Indians' benefactor, instructing them in agriculture and the arts of government. Banished because he had incurred the wrath of a principal deity, he promised before embarking from the shores of the Gulf of Mexico that he and his descendants would return one day. We also learn that: "He was said to have been tall in stature, with a white skin, long, dark hair, and a flowing beard. The Mexicans looked confidently to the return of the benevolent deity; and this remarkable tradition, deeply cherished in their hearts, prepared the way, as we shall see hereafter, for the future success of the Spaniards." (I, 73)

The power of the Aztec priesthood and its fanatical commitment to the gods, which prolonged the agony of the final struggle against the Spaniards, are described here, as are the *teocallis* (pyramids), where later the Spaniards unfortunate enough to be captured alive were sacrificed. Also included in this third chapter is a detailed description of the ritual of sacrifice, one of the most impressive passages in the entire history. On the summit of the pyramid, the victim was received by six priests who

led him to the sacrificial stone, a huge block of jasper, with its upper surface somewhat convex. On this the prisoner was stretched. Five priests secured his head and his limbs; while the sixth, clad in a scarlet mantle, emblematic of his bloody office, dexterously opened the breast of the wretched victim with a sharp razor of *itztli,* — a volcanic substance, hard as flint, — and, inserting his hand in the wound, tore out the palpitating heart. The minister of death, first holding this up towards the sun, an object of worship throughout Anahuac, cast it at the feet of the deity to whom the temple was devoted, while the multitudes below prostrated themselves in humble adoration. (I, 91)

The body of the sacrificed victim, we later learn, was "delivered to the warrior who had taken him in battle, and by him, after being dressed, was served up in an entertainment to his friends" (I, 93). While Prescott discounts the high Spanish figures (twenty thousand to fifty thousand) for the number of victims sacrificed, he believes it safe to conclude that thousands were sacrificed annually to the Mexican gods. Prescott's conclusion to the chapter, which places both it and the yet to be narrated conquest in perspective, develops the grand design of the history: "In this state of things it was beneficently ordered by Providence that the land should be delivered over to another race, who would rescue it from the brutish superstitions that daily extended wider and wider with extent of empire." (I, 101)

The survey of Mexican hieroglyphics, manuscripts, chronology, and astronomy was the most difficult chapter in the history to write. "A hard, barren topic," Prescott notes in the *Memoranda* after finishing the notes for the hieroglyphical part of the chapter: "am now on the astronomy — frying pan into the fire" (II, 52). Yet he mastered both subjects, for his explanations are lucid. We have defined for us the kinds of hieroglyphical writing (representational, symbolical, and phonetic) and the difference between the Egyptian and inferior Aztec systems. Equally clear, and far more impressive, is Prescott's explanation of the Aztec chronology, whose system of intercalation brought their year within two minutes and nine seconds of the exact length of the tropical year. "We cannot contemplate the astronomical science of the Mexicans, so disproportionate to their progress in other walks of civilization, without astonishment" (I, 138). This chapter, together with the fifth, where we learn of their husbandry and skill in metalwork and witness one of their social entertainments, modifies the picture of the Aztecs as a race totally committed to war and sacrifice.

A narrative account of the golden age of the Tezcucans, a neighboring nation rivaling the Aztecs in power and surpassing them in culture, concludes the history of the Mexican civilization. In their monarch, Nezahualcoyotl, who rises from hunted prince to powerful ruler, Prescott found a focus for the sixth chapter. The fifteen-year-old prince's flight after witnessing his father's murder by the invading Tepanecs, his subsequent hairbreadth escapes, his hiding in caves and thickets, the loyalty of the Tezcucans who endured torture and death rather than betray him, and his eventual return to his throne after leading a coalition force against the Tepanecs — all are the elements of the narrative.

In the second half of the chapter Prescott shows the Tezcucan golden age to be a direct result of Nezahualcoyotl's energetic and forceful rule. The government was remodeled, a comprehensive code of law was formed, and the arts and sciences were encouraged. More impressive was the monarch's repudiation of the rite of human sacrifice that the Tezcucans had borrowed from the Aztecs. Though he could not abolish the practice, he restricted the victims to slaves and captives. His more positive act was to build a temple to "the Unknown God, the Cause of Causes," and to forbid either image or blood sacrifice to profane it. For one act only, Prescott tempers his eulogy of the king: "Thus died the greatest monarch, and if one foul blot could be effaced, perhaps the best, that ever sat upon an Indian throne" (I, 213). Enamored of a maiden betrothed to one of his vassals, the king had ordered the nobleman into the thickest part of battle where he lost his life.

The history of the Tezcucans concludes with the account of their decline under Nezahualcoyotl's son Nezahualpilli, whom the Aztec sovereign Montezuma plundered of some of his most valuable domains and supplanted as head of the Mexican alliance. As for the Tezcucans themselves:

> . . . they had begun in the right way, and already showed a refinement in sentiment and manners, a capacity for receiving instruction, which, under good auspices, might have led them on to indefinite improvement. Unhappily, they were fast falling under the dominion of the warlike Aztecs. And that people repaid the benefits received from their more polished neighbors by imparting to them their own ferocious superstition, which, falling like a mildew on the land, would soon have blighted its rich blossoms of promise and turned even its fruits to dust and ashes. (I, 220)

Strategically placed as it is at the conclusion of the history of the Mexican civilization, this passage becomes an implicit justification for the conquest. The stage was now set.

III   *Conquest*

The conquest of Mexico was a campaign conducted far differently from the war of Granada. Whereas the war was sanctioned by the Church and fought by chivalry led by the Spanish monarchs themselves, the conquest was an unauthorized expedition undertaken by adventurers led by a brilliant and daring soldier of fortune. Consequently the expedition was threatened not only by the native population of Mexico but also by undisciplined and dissatisfied men within the ranks and by jealous and ambitious Spaniards organizing in Hispaniola to overtake and depose the expedition's leader. The effects of these factors on the expedition become evident in the following outline of the conquest:

Flight from Cuba. Aware that Velasquez, the governor of Cuba, contemplates rescinding his commission as Captain-General of the expedition to the Mexican mainland, Cortés with his volunteer forces sails from Santiago by night. With a force of 553 soldiers, 110 mariners, 200 Indians, and 16 horses, he lands on the Yucatán peninsula on February 18, 1519.

Founding of Vera Cruz. Holding no warranty from Velasquez to colonize or penetrate farther into the interior of Mexico, Cortés settles a colony *in the name of the Spanish sovereigns.* With the authority of Velasquez now superseded by the magistry of Villa Rica de Vera Cruz, Cortés manages to be reappointed Captain-General and Chief Justice *of the colony.* "By this ingenious transformation of a military into a civil community, he had secured a new and effectual basis for future operations." (II, 33)

Destruction of the Fleet. After detecting a conspiracy among some of the men to seize a vessel and return to Cuba, Cortés recognizes that so long as a means of escape remains, desertion will be a constant threat. Circulating the false report that sea worms have eaten into the sides and bottoms of the ships, he orders the sails, cordage, and iron removed and the ships sunk.

Defeat of the Tlascalans. The Spaniards meet their first formidable Indian foe, the Tlascalans, the "Swiss of Anahuac," a nation that has successfully resisted the Aztec invasion of their land. Defeated by the Spaniards in a series of fierce battles, they become Cortés' staunchest ally against the Aztecs.

Massacre at Cholula. At Cholula, within a hundred miles of the Mexican capital, the Spaniards are graciously received by the inhabitants of the city. A few days later Cortés discovers that the Cholulans and a force of twenty thousand Aztecs waiting nearby plan to fall on the Spaniards as they leave the city. On the morning following the discovery of the plot, the Spaniards attack the Cholulans, killing some six thousand of the male population before Cortés calls off the soldiers.

On November 8, 1519 the Spaniards enter the Mexican capital unopposed and are welcomed by Montezuma who, strangely enough, had not committed the Aztec nation to battle against the invaders.

Seizure of Montezuma. In the capital only a week, Cortés realizes how perilous his position is. To secure himself against an Aztec uprising and buy time to conquer the city before a superior force from Cuba can supplant him, Cortés seizes Montezuma and imprisons him in the Spanish quarters.

The Attack on Narvaez. Learning that Velasquez has sent a force under the command of Narvaez to replace him, Cortés leaves Alvarado in charge of the capital and marches with 266 men to engage his new enemy (900 men, 80 horses, and 1,000 Indians). During a driving rainstorm he makes a surprise attack on Narvaez who has taken shelter in the city of Cempoalla. Victorious, he enlists Narvaez's men under his banner.

While at Cempoalla Cortés learns that the Mexicans are in arms and have attacked his garrison in the capital. By the time he reaches the city, the Mexicans have stopped their attack and are attempting a blockade, but the Spaniards are able to enter the city unopposed. Fighting soon begins again, but the Spaniards are unprepared for the ferocity and military efficiency of the Aztecs.

Storming of the Great Pyramid. A short distance from the Spanish garrison stands the great *teocalli* (pyramid) of the war god, Huitzilopochtli, from which the Mexicans rain arrows down on the Spaniards. Since the Spaniards must dislodge them, Cortés himself leads the storming party that fights its way to the summit in a battle lasting three hours and covering nearly a mile as it moves around the pyramid.

Despite this victory, the Spaniards realize that they must evacuate the city, since the Aztecs have increased their attacks, the Spanish forces are diminishing, and their provisions are becoming dangerously low. With the death of Montezuma, they no longer have a hostage.

The Noche Triste ("melancholy night"). As the Spaniards sneak out of the city by night across the broken causeway of Tlacopan, they are discovered by the Aztecs and a terrible slaughter occurs. The number of Spaniards killed and missing is four hundred and that of their Indian allies four thousand.

The Battle of Otumba. At Otumba, nine leagues from the capital, Cortés finds his retreat to Tlascala blocked by a huge Mexican force. Unable to retreat, "he must . . . cut through the enemy, or perish" (III, 196). The battle is desperate, and the tide is rapidly turning against the Spaniards when Cortés, detecting at a distance the commander of the Aztecs, calls to his cavalry to follow him. They cut their way through the Mexicans to the Indian commander whom Cortés strikes to the ground — an act that precipitates a panic among the Indians and gives the victory to the Spaniards.

After five months in the Republic of Tlascala where adventurers from Cuba have swelled the number of Spaniards under arms to six hundred, Cortés sets out again for Mexico, this time to conquer. He will establish headquarters at Tezcuco near Lake Tezcuco, in whose center stands the Mexican capital and whose waters he will command with the thirteen brigantines built at Tlascala and transported twenty leagues across the mountains.

Conspiracy in the Army. While at Tezcuco, Cortés detects a conspiracy against his life and those of his most trusted officers by a party unwilling to face the dangers involved in the forthcoming march against the capital. Because he needs every man, he pretends not to know the identities of the conspirators and executes only the ringleader.

Siege and Conquest of Mexico. Gaining control of Lake Tezcuco with his fleet, Cortés begins the real conquest of Mexico, this time fighting his way into the city, where the fighting advances street by street and house by house until the Mexicans capitulate.

IV *Emphasis*

Prescott develops his narrative of the conquest with the kind of facts, descriptions, and anecdotes that made the history the most martial and suspenseful he ever wrote. He constantly reminds the reader of the size of the Spanish force, a pitifully small one for the task its leader had proposed for it. At Tlascala, for example, four hundred Spanish foot and fifteen horse, with three thousand Indian allies, encounter a Tlascalan force of over fifty thousand. Even when Cortés doubles his forces, he cannot reduce his odds. Against the entire Aztec nation in the final struggle for Mexico, he can throw only eight hundred Spanish foot and eighty-seven horses.[10] More impressive than the numerical odds are the consequences of a Spanish defeat, which Prescott has the Aztecs describe for the invaders' edification: "Huitzilopochtli has long cried for his victims. The stone of sacrifice is ready. The knives are sharpened. The wild beasts in the palace are roaring for their offal" (III, 119). That "despair gave unnatural energy to [the Spaniard's] arm" (II, 136) is not, then, a rhetorical flourish.

However, desperation alone, Prescott recognizes, did not wholly account for the succession of Spanish victories. They resulted from the impact and interrelationship of tactics, armament, the horse, superstition and the opponent: "The naked body of the Indian afforded no resistance to the sharp Toledo steel" (II, 137). The Tlascalans "were too deficient in military science to profit by their vast superiority in numbers. . . . They knew not how to concentrate numbers on a given point, or even how to sustain an assault, by employing successive detachments to support and relieve one another" (II, 137). The Indians were thrown into further confusion by the Spanish artillery and cavalry: "The nations of Anahuac had no large domestic animals, and were unacquainted with any beast of burden. Their imaginations were bewildered when they beheld the strange apparition of the horse and his rider moving in unison and obedient to one impulse, as if possessed of a common nature" (II, 140).

No such awe, however, invested the captured Spaniard, whose sacrifice to the Aztec war god Prescott records in detail: after the heart, "which, hot and reeking, was deposited on the golden censer

before the idol . . . the mutilated remains were gathered up by the
savages beneath, who soon prepared them with the cannibal repast
which completed the work of abomination!" (IV, 53). It is no
wonder, then, that each encounter between the European and the
Indian holds such high drama and suspense. In *Ferdinand and
Isabella*, where Christians fought with Christians or highly civilized
infidels, capture meant imprisonment with provision for ransom of
the nobility, or at worst, consignment to the galleys. In *Mexico* the
shadow of the convex sacrificial stone and knife-wielding priest
hovered over every battlefield.

V   *Battles*

"Not easy to describe so much blood & thunder with variety,"
Prescott wrote of his account of the battle at Tlascala. "Wars of barbarians don't admit of the animated interest & description growing
out of the evolutions & counter-workings of a refined military
science. Brute masses, brute force — *voilà tout.* — Still some room
for the *picturesque*" (*Memoranda*, II, 79). Yet the battles in *Mexico*
are far more varied than the author's account of the successive sieges
that make up the conquest of Granada. The struggle on the
causeway during the *noche triste*, for example, contrasts drastically
with the storming of the Great Pyramid where Cortés and his
followers must fight their way to its summit for their final encounter
with its defenders. On that "aerial battle-field," its edge un-
protected by parapet or battlement, "the least slip would be fatal;
and the combatants, as they struggled in mortal agony, were
sometimes seen to roll over the sheer sides of the precipice
together." (III, 130 - 31)

The battle during the *noche triste* is quite different. While
attempting to escape from the capital over the broken causeway, the
Spaniards were attacked by the Aztecs. Unable to cross the breach
before them because their portable wooden bridge had become
wedged behind them, the trapped Spaniards were thrown into
confusion:

The leading files, urged on by the rear, were crowded on the brink of the
gulf . . . some, who reached the opposite bank, being overturned in the as-
cent, rolled headlong with their steeds into the lake. The infantry followed
pellmell, heaped promiscuously on one another, frequently pierced by the
shafts or struck down by the war-clubs of the Aztecs; while many an unfortunate victim was dragged half stunned on board their canoes, to be
reserved for a protracted but more dreadful death. (III, 167)

At Otumba, where the wide field afforded room for the effective use of cavalry, the battle's turning point came with a desperate charge led by Cortés and a handful of his cavaliers against the Aztec commander. The battles on Lake Tezcuco between the brigantines and the Aztecs in their canoes provide further variety in the account of the fighting. Finally, in the invasion of the capital, where the fighting was street by street, Prescott demonstrates a point he made repeatedly: ". . . entangled in the long streets and narrow lanes of the metropolis, where every house was a citadel, the Spaniards, as experience had shown, would lose much of their superiority" (III, 314). It finally became necessary to level the buildings and fill the canals and breaches so that the cavalry could maneuver. Each battle, then, was as different as its site, and the author's account of it varies accordingly. History itself had provided Prescott with the variety needed to maintain interest in the series of struggles between Europeans and "barbarians" in the New World. But it is ultimately the author who makes those battles distinct and memorable, losing nothing in the blur of attacks, counterattacks, and hand-to-hand combat that characterized those encounters.

VI   *Cortés*

Given the odds the Spaniards faced, the characters of the men themselves, and the complete lack of support by the Spanish crown, it is surprising that the conquest was undertaken at all. More surprising, though, is that a man emerged who not only had the temerity to lead such an expedition but who also could carry it to a successful conclusion. *The Conquest of Mexico* has a clearly defined thesis which its author relentlessly demonstrates (to the thorough enjoyment of the reader): Cortés was the body and the soul of the conquest (IV, 251).

After a brief biography of his protagonist before his departure for Mexico, Prescott sets the stage for the drama. Appointed by Velasquez, the governor of Cuba, to explore the coast of Mexico and barter with the Indians, Cortés learned that the jealous governor planned to replace him. He embarked immediately, shouting his farewells from an armed boat to the governor who had galloped to the quay to stop him. Thus we are prepared from the outset for one of the problems that would plague the conqueror — fear of recall from command of the expedition or attack by a superior force from Hispaniola or Cuba. Even after he was safely inside the Mexican capital, Cortés could not assume that his mission was legitimate. His envoys to Charles V had reached that monarch when Charles had just learned of his election to the imperial crown of Germany. In the midst of preparations for leaving Spain, Charles was not interested in the affairs of the New World and departed without settling the dispute between Cortés and Velasquez, an act duly commented on by Prescott: "What a contrast to the policy of his illustrious predecesors, Ferdinand and Isabella!" (III, 29)

Cortés' immediate concern, however, was maintaining discipline and morale within his small force. Given the dangers and privations the men faced, the heat and venomous insects, the commander's task was made even more difficult by the character of his followers, "soldiers of fortune . . . [who] regarded their captain — the captain of a day — as little more than an equal" (II, 24). In Cortés' ability to control such men, Prescott finds the touchstone of his hero's character. Aware that his men were "rough and turbulent spirits, who required to be ruled with an iron hand" (III, 257), he made no attempt to repress the familiarity that had developed between them and their officers who had shared the perils and sufferings of the expedition:

But the limits of his forbearance were clearly defined; and any attempt to overstep them, or to violate the established regulations of the camp, brought a sure and speedy punishment on the offender. By thus tempering severity with indulgence, masking an iron will under the open bearing of a soldier, Cortés established a control over his band of bold and reckless adventurers, such as a pedantic martinet, scrupulous in enforcing the minutiae of military etiquette, could never have obtained. (III, 257 - 58)

This control was so sure, Prescott shows, that even after suffering serious reverses, Cortés could win the men to a firmer allegiance by actually inviting them to desert him: "Let them leave their general in his extremity. He should feel stronger in the service of a few brave spirits than if surrounded by a host of the false or the faint-hearted." (III, 215)

Prescott makes us realize that for all Cortés' personal force and skill in instilling the desire for glory in his men none of these would have availed him had he not been preeminent as a soldier. Throughout the history he is in the forefront of all the action: "Amidst the din of battle at Tlascala, the voice of Cortés was heard, cheering on his soldiers. . . . Animated by the words and heroic bearing of their general, the soldiers . . . succeeded in forcing a passage

through the dark columns of the enemy" (II, 123). Similar passages
appear in the accounts of the fighting at the Great Pyramid, on the
causeway, and at Otumba.

With these anecdotes and descriptions of the leader, there are the
author's own assessments, sometimes metaphorical or highly subjective, but always appropriate and vivid: "There are some hardy
natures that require the heats of excited action to unfold their
energies; like the plants which, closed to the mild influence of a
temperate latitude, come to their full growth, and give forth their
fruits, only in the burning atmosphere of the tropics" (I, 326). In
other passages Prescott has so closely empathized with his hero that
he freely interpolates thoughts he believes appropriate to him. For
example, when Cortés beholds the remnant of his bewildered and
demoralized followers after the slaughter of the *noche triste* and contemplates his loss of men and reputation and the serious problem of
survival in a land no longer convinced of Spanish invulnerability,
Prescott writes:

Yet these agitating and gloomy reflections, which might have crushed a
common mind, had no power over that of Cortés; or, rather, they only
served to renew his energies and quicken his perceptions, as the war of the
elements purifies and gives elasticity to the atmosphere. . . . In the very hour
of discomfiture and general despondency, there is no doubt that his heroic
spirit was meditating the plan of operations which he afterwards pursued
with such dauntless constancy. (III, 178 - 79)

It is difficult to fault the subjective element in the passage when
history has borne out the author's interpolation.

VII *Antagonist*

The worst policy to adopt when dealing with such a man is vacillation, the policy adopted by the person history chose to cast as Cortés'
antagonist. Montezuma, influenced by the legend of his people —
that Quetzalcoatl would return someday — saw in the Spanish invaders " ' the men of destiny' who were to take possession of his
sceptre" (II, 159). While others of his military claque called for the
annihilation of the invaders, the emperor, confused by events and
his counselors, chose what Prescott terms "a half-way course, — as
usual, the most impolitic" and sent an embassy with both magnificent presents and orders forbidding the Spaniards to approach the
capital. "This was to reveal at once both his wealth and weakness"
(II, 14). When the Spaniards had crossed the mountains and were in

the Valley of Mexico, there was still time for defense. "But the monarch found it difficult to rally his spirits for this final struggle. . . . He would have acted a more glorious part had he put his capital in a posture of defence, and prepared, like the last of the Palaeologi, to bury himself under its ruins." (II, 236)

In concluding that Montezuma acted cowardly, Prescott attributes his behavior to his belief in the Spaniards' divinity. Yet as David Levin has observed, if Montezuma sincerely believed that the Spaniards were really the white gods of prophecy (and Prescott nowhere suggests that he did not believe it), then he followed his religious beliefs and bowed to the inevitable. Whatever Montezuma's motivation, he was by his fate (ignoble capture by the Spaniards and humiliation by his own people, which destroyed his will to live) "the sad victim of destiny."

VIII   *Point of View*

As in *Ferdinand and Isabella,* there is the impressive authorial commentary that establishes the presence of a strong personality behind the writing. The point of view is still moral and progressive, and the tendency is to philosophize when the morality of an action seems questionable. Cortés' ordering the hands of the fifty Tlascalan spies cut off was a customary punishment of the time, we are told. If we are revolted by the decree, "we should reflect that it was . . . not more uncommon, indeed, than whipping and branding with a hot iron were in our own country" in later time. Although "a higher civilization . . . rejects such punishments, as pernicious in themselves, . . . it is too much to ask of any man, still less one bred to the iron trade of war, to be in advance of the refinement of his age" (II, 155).

This practice of assessing events from a consistently moral and progressive point of view ultimately distinguishes *The Conquest of Mexico* from an artistic fusion of facts and romantic narrative and transforms it into a memorable history. Nowhere is that assessment more vivid or necessary than at the conclusion of the narrative of the conquest. Noting that the fall of an empire "which did so little to promote the happiness of its subjects or the real interests of humanity" is no cause for regret, Prescott scores the brutality of the Mexicans: "The Aztecs not only did not advance the condition of their vassals, but, morally speaking, they did much to degrade it. How can a nation where human sacrifices prevail, and especially when combined with cannibalism, further the march of civilization?" (IV, 112 - 13). "The empire of the Aztecs," he concludes, "did not fall before its time" (IV, 114).

The narrative continues with Cortés' subsequent career, which could not match the brilliance of his life up to and including the conquest. Cortés suffered disappointment and rejection. At one point he was forbidden to approach within ten leagues of Mexico; there was a cool reception by Charles V and an abortive expedition to Algiers.

Prescott faced squarely the danger of anticlimax but he had the good judgment to keep the post-conquest account brief. Granted that there is a falling off of interest in this portion of the history, the falling off is inconsequential, given the fascination and suspense generated by the real subject of the work, the march to Mexico, "the greatest miracle in an age of miracles," in Prescott's opinion.

"Epic in prose," "a romance of chivalry," "the most poetic subject ever offered to the pen of the historian" — these are the phrases in the *Memoranda* describing the true way of conceiving the conquest of Mexico. How would the author conceive another story of a conquest?

CHAPTER 6

"Quarrels of Banditti over the Spoils"

O N April 23, 1845 Prescott made the following entry in the *Literary Memoranda*, regarding the progress of his current history, *The Conquest of Peru:*

> The story may be arranged so as to produce a striking & picturesque narrative. But its great defect is want of unity. The action of the piece properly terminates with the reduction of Cuzco — & the subversion of the empire of the Incas, — and that is before the story is half ended, — the rest — civil dissensions among the Conquerors, Fine passages of insulated beauty — touches of character — dashing exploits — marvellous adventure — oceans of gold — appalling cruelties — heroic endurance — but mixed up with unintermitting ferocity & cupidity — low aiming & bad faith — vulgar passions & license of every description, from which the mind turns away in disgust. (II, 142)

In later entries it became further evident that *The Conquest of Peru* would not be the epic its predecessor had been.[1] History itself had precluded that possibility.

Since comparisons between the two histories are inevitable, we should account for the differences between them. First, as Prescott explains, the two cultures were quite different: "In the most degrading feature of the moral character of the Aztecs, in religious worship, the Peruvian has an immense advantage — bloodless rites, & homage to deities having no stain — the worship of an overruling Creature — and that of the heavenly bodies." Consequently, Prescott noted, he would not get from "the uniform, tame, & *mould-like* character & institutions of the Incas" the striking and picturesque effects provided him by the contrast in the extremes of civilization and barbarism in the Aztecs (II, 119 -20). Furthermore, such a people would be deficient in military organization and thus could not offer effective resistance against a determined foe.

The second difference between the two histories, something "deficient in point of character among the conquerors," was noted early by Adolphe de Circourt in a letter to the historian. Prescott did not put the matter quite as delicately in his own correspondence: "Pray do if you can pick up some family arms of the Pizarros for an ornament to my next volumes. They were I fear such unmitigated ruffians that they should have had no arms but a butcher's cleaver."[2] After the death of the Inca Atahuallpa, the history, he noted in the *Memoranda*, "is but a second rate — quarrels of banditti over the spoils." Later he concluded that "the feuds of these civilized barbarians have little interest or profit."

As would be expected, Prescott explicitly comments on the differences between the leaders of the two conquests:

Indeed, Pizarro seems to have had the example of his great predecessor before his eyes on more occasions than this. But he fell far short of his model; for, notwithstanding the restraint he sometimes put upon himself, his coarser nature and more ferocious temper often betrayed him into acts most repugnant to sound policy, which would never have been countenanced by the Conqueror of Mexico (VI, 33 - 34).[3]

In the obituary of Pizarro which Prescott wrote, we learn that, while Cortés displayed profound policy in enlisting conflicting nations under his banner and conducted his campaign with admirable tactics and strategy, the conqueror of Peru "appears only as an adventurer, a fortunate knight-errant"; further, he "was eminently perfidious." With such a figure for his protagonist, Prescott's talents for creating epic adventure were sorely tested.

They were tested even more by the events of the conquest, more specifically by the order in which they occurred, for in regard to the conquest of Peru, history itself is anticlimactic. "The reduction of Peru might now be considered as in a manner accomplished," Prescott wrote with still a volume and a half of the history to be written. In the first chapter of the third volume the conqueror is murdered and the history becomes a study of a half-dozen Spanish leaders of differing ability and character. Given this order of events, the character of the conquerors and the nature of the civilization overthrown, we must conclude that *The Conquest of Peru* is in many ways a triumph over the materials provided it by history.

I   *Form*

Prescott divides the history into five books: the first, a "View of the Civilization of the Incas"; the second, the "Discovery of Peru";

the third, the "Conquest of Peru"; the fourth, the "Civil Wars of the Conquerors"; and the fifth, "Settlement of the Country." The first book is similar to the "Introduction to the Aztec Civilization" in its topical arrangement. There is a chapter on the physical aspects and products of Peru and a history of the Incas, followed by chapters on civil institutions, religion, astrology, sciences, and the arts.[4] It is a careful study, Prescott perhaps being particularly diligent in this portion of the work to compensate for the quality of the narrative that would follow:

The narrative of the Conquest will not be as stirring in events, or as *epical* in its conduct — as the Mexican. But I do not see why the Introduction should not contain as much matter of interest to the student of his species, and present a picture if not so striking, — full as novel, & much more pleasing to dwell on." (*Memoranda*, II, 125)

As in the "Introduction to the Mexican Civilization," he concludes the account with a series of reflections: " . . . we cannot but be struck with the total dissimilarity between these institutions and those of the Aztecs" (V, 179), he writes, noting especially their differences in military policy and religious systems. Whereas the Aztecs carried on wars of extermination and ended their ceremonies with human sacrifices and cannibal orgies, the Peruvians preferred negotiation and intrigue to violence, and they rarely practiced human sacrifice. Prescott is more impressed, however, with the absolute power of the Inca who was "both the lawgiver and the law." "Not merely the representative of Divinity . . . he was Divinity itself." (V, 185)

Prescott indicates that such a system of government was the most despotic though the mildest of despotisms the world had ever seen. Every aspect of the Peruvian's life was regulated by law. If he never knew poverty or neglect, he also never knew "the power of free agency — the inestimable and inborn right of every human being" (V, 187). The defeat of such a people by the militant forces of progress was inevitable since "the spirit of independence could hardly be strong in a people who had no interest in the soil, no personal rights to defend" (V, 192). But as David Levin has observed, Prescott does not settle the difficult question of the right of conquest, since the population consisted not of warlike Aztecs but of industrious and peaceful farmers, artisans, and worshippers of the Sun.[5]

II *Conquest and Civil Wars*

The account of the conquest itself, as the following summary shows, lacks the unity that characterized *The Conquest of Mexico.* Its main object — the fall of the Inca empire — is accomplished midway in the history.

After two harrowing, exploratory voyages along the coasts of Ecuador and Peru to the ninth latitude, Francisco Pizarro returns to Panama where he and his associate in the enterprise, Diego de Almagro, agree that Pizarro must apply to the crown for help in the expedition to Peru. In the spring of 1528 he sails to Spain, taking with him some natives, as well as three llamas, articles of cloth, and ornaments of gold and silver. In Spain he is granted the right of discovery and conquest in the province of New Castile (Peru), in addition to the title and rank of Governor and Captain-General of the province for life. Gonzalo, Juan, and Hernando Pizarro, half brothers of the conqueror, return to the New World with him. In January 1531 Pizarro, leading a force of 180 men and 27 horses, leaves the Bay of Panama for the third and last expedition for the conquest of Peru. They will be joined later by Almagro and reinforcements.

The Spaniards arrive in Peru just at the end of an important war. On his deathbed the Inca had given the ancient kingdom of Quito to his favorite son, Atahuallpa. The rest of the empire he left to the legitimate successor, his older son Huascar who would rule at Cuzco. Now, five years later, war had broken out and the army of Atahuallpa had taken Cuzco and captured Huascar. The Spaniards, having landed at the Isle of Punta, enter South America at Tumbas and after a severe passage across the Andes encounter Atahuallpa encamped with a large army at Caxamalca (Cajamarca).

Recognizing how perilous their position is — they are vastly outnumbered and too far in the interior to receive help — they decide that their only hope is to take the Inca prisoner. They invite him to visit them in Caxamalca where they are quartered. With his retinue, Atahuallpa enters the city where he is informed by the Spaniards that he must recognize Charles V as his sovereign and accept the Catholic faith. When he refuses to become a vassal, he is seized. His retinue, numbering in the thousands, is slaughtered.

The story of his ransom is well known. Learning of his captors' greed for gold, Atahuallpa promises to fill a room seventeen by twenty-two feet to a height of nine feet with gold if they will free him. Before that mark is reached rumors of an Indian uprising reach the Spaniards, who cannot risk its being led by an Inca god. Accordingly they charge their prisoner with idolatry and with attempting to incite an insurrection against them. The Inca is sentenced to be burned at the stake, but upon his conversion to Christianity, the sentence is commuted to death by garroting.

Joined by Almagro and his men, Pizarro takes Cuzco unopposed, thereby completing the conquest of Peru. Leaving Almagro at Cuzco, he moves on to Rimac (Lima) to establish the new capital of the colonial empire. In the meantime, Almagro, preparing to undertake the conquest of Chile, learns of a large land grant awarded him by Charles V and assumes that Cuzco is part of it, a major cause of friction between the two commanders. When Hernando Pizarro, sent to occupy Cuzco in Almagro's absence, allows the puppet Inca, Manco Capac, to escape, the Indians rally and besiege the city, providing the bloodiest fighting between Europeans and Indians in the entire history. Finding the city besieged when he returns from Chile, Almagro drives the Indians away and imprisons Gonzalo and Hernando Pizarro. Negotiations and fighting follow, ending with the defeat and execution of Almagro, an event that concludes the first civil war of the conquerors and establishes the complete authority of the Pizarros in Peru.

The peace, however, is short-lived. Having gathered in Lima, the followers of Almagro and his son, Diego, impoverished by their loss of lands and despairing of any redress from Spain, break into the governor's palace and assassinate the conqueror of Peru. The younger Almagro and his followers, who have now grown in numbers, are, in turn, defeated in a fierce battle by Vaca de Castro, an officer from Spain carrying a royal commission empowering him to assume the government. No sooner has the young Almagro been executed at Cuzco than de Castro learns that Gonzalo Pizarro is in Lima with his forces and is contemplating seizing the government. Summoned to Cuzco by de Castro, Gonzalo relinquishes for the time being his claim to the government.

In this turbulent arena an unfortunate choice of Viceroy appears. Blasco Nuñez Vela, precipitate and unperceptive, has been sent from Spain to enforce humanitarian reforms which would, in effect, make the Indians free men. Because the reforms would also deprive the Spaniards of their workers, and consequently their wealth, their enforcement by the high-handed viceroy soon throws the country into turmoil. In Lima, Gonzalo Pizarro is proclaimed Governor and Captain-General of Peru, "till his Majesty's pleasure could be known in respect to the government" (VII, 117). With the subsequent death of Blasco Nuñez Vela in battle and Vaca de Castro's return to Spain, he becomes master in Peru.

News of these events prompts Philip II, who is governing Spain during his father's absence in Germany, to call a council to decide on a course of action. To land a large army and send it into the interior when the ports and roads are held by rebels is impractical if not impossible. Conciliatory measures would have to be tried, and an agent capable of making concessions to the Pizarro faction "without too far compromising the dignity and permanent authority of the crown" (VII, 164) would have to be found. This agent is Pedro de la Gasca, an ecclesiastic who was distinguished by his scholarship, discretion, and loyalty to the crown. He also "possessed an acquaintance with affairs, and even with military science, such as was to have been expected only from one reared in courts and camps." (VII, 168)

Invested with powers to meet any emergency he might encounter in Peru, Gasca embarks with a slender train of followers for the New World on May 26, 1546. By his bearing and unusual good sense in dealing with those officers committed to Gonzalo, he is able to win many back to the crown. Though his force under Centeno is badly beaten at Huarina, Gasca resolutely moves to engage the rebels at Xaquixaguana near Cuzco, his ranks swelled by the constant arrival of reinforcements.

Before the battle can begin, there are wholesale desertions to the Royalists, and Pizarro and the few officers who remain by him have no choice but to surrender. With their execution, the last threat to Spanish control of Peru ends. Gasca soon begins work to place the authority of the crown on a permanent basis; and, when he leaves Peru in January, 1550, he has accomplished the great object of his mission: Peru is firmly secured to the Spanish crown.

III   Craft and Tactics

The Conquest of Peru represents an author's triumph over his materials. Prescott had to observe chronology, and he was obligated to depict men as they were, not as he would have preferred them. Aware from the outset of the anticlimax in the history, the lack of dramatic unity, and the limitations of the protagonist and antagonists, he exploits to the fullest any opportunities for dramatic effects that history might provide him. Fortunately, the events and men involved elicited from him that quality of writing which had distinguished the earlier histories.

The seizure of Atahuallpa, for example, provides Prescott with the kind of action he could invest with high drama. The preparation for the act, its logic, and its execution replete with vivid anecdotes are treated in detail. Vastly outnumbered by the Inca's forces at Cax-amalca, the Spaniards lack an escape route. "Whither could they fly? At the first signal of retreat, the whole army of the Inca would be upon them." But if they remained long in their present position, "familiarity with the white men would soon destroy the idea of any thing supernatural, or even superior, in their natures." Their only remedy, then, was to seize Atahuallpa. "With the Inca once in his power, Pizarro might dictate laws to the empire." (VI, 102 - 104)

There follows an incredible confrontation in the square of Cax-amalca between Atahuallpa and Father Valverde who beseeches the Inca to embrace Christianity and become a vassal of Charles V. Atahuallpa flings down the Bible the priest has presented as his authority and demands an account of the Spaniards' presence in his land, an act that precipitates the end of his reign:

The friar, greatly scandalized by the indignity offered to the sacred volume, stayed only to pick it up, and, hastening to Pizarro, informed him of what had been done, exclaiming, at the same time, "Do you not see that while we stand here wasting our breath in talking with this dog, full of pride as he is, the fields are filling with Indians? Set on at once; I absolve you." Pizarro saw that the hour had come. He waved a white scarf in the air, the appointed signal. The fatal gun was fired from the fortress. Then, springing into the square, the Spanish captain and his followers shouted the old war-cry of "St. Jago and at them." It was answered by the battle-cry of every Spaniard in the city, as, rushing from the avenues of the great halls in which they were concealed, they poured into the *plaza*, horse and foot, each in his own dark column, and threw themselves into the midst of the Indian crowd. (VI, 117)

Also memorable is Gonzalo Pizarro's expedition to the Amazon, "an expedition which, for its dangers and hardships, the length of their duration, and the constancy with which they were endured, stands perhaps unmatched in the annals of American discovery" (VI, 385). Three hundred and fifty Spaniards and four thousand Indians make the arduous passage across the Andes to the Amazon. After an earthquake, six weeks of heavy rain, famine, desertion, and death take their toll, more than half of the Indians perish, and only eighty of the Spaniards survive the four-hundred league journey back to Quito. That any returned, Prescott establishes, was due to the resolute leadership of Gonzalo.

Always interested in military strategy, Prescott found in the conflicts between the Spaniards themselves another source for the kind of descriptive writing he enjoyed most. Here in *Peru* he would have the opportunity for the first time to describe the use of firearms as an important tactical weapon. In Mexico and against the Peruvians, their effect had been primarily psychological, but in the civil wars they were used by and against trained soldiers deployed by skilled commanders who judged their effect by the number of casualties they inflicted. On the plains outside Huarina, situated on the southeastern shore of Lake Titicaca, superior firepower and tactics decided the issue between a larger force of Royalists and the rebel army of Gonzalo Pizarro. With its careful description of the opposing armies, their armament and alignment, the account is characteristic of Prescott's other narratives of formal battles where the reader, as though he were provided with a map and battle plan, comprehends immediately the strategy and combat as they develop.

First the rebel center, composed of pikemen and infantrymen armed with two or more arquebuses, calmly await the advance of the Royalist foot to within sixty paces of their line before opening a devastating fire that puts them to rout. They then receive the charge of the Royalist cavalry, which is "unable to break through the dense array of pikes, held by the steady hands of troops who stood firm and fearless on their post" (VII, 220). The cavalry charge on the rebel rear proves even more disastrous:

[The] men facing about with the promptness and discipline of well-trained soldiers, the rear was converted into the front. The same forest of spears was presented to the attack; while an incessant discharge of balls punished the audacity of the cavaliers, who, broken and completely dispirited by their ineffectual attempt, at length imitated the example of the panic-struck foot and abandoned the field. (VII, 221)

The reader coming to the battle at Huarina from the Italian Wars of *Ferdinand and Isabella* recognizes an evolution in military science. The pike of the Swiss and their hedgehog tactic that had been adopted by the Spaniards in Italy have now been joined with the arquebus in Peru to confound Spanish chivalry.

IV *Conqueror*

While accounts such as these add immeasurably to the interest of *Peru*, those historical facts which preclude an artistically unified narrative remain: anticlimax, an almost too-civilized native population, a ruffian band of adventurers, an illiterate and cruel commander. Had the leader been a man of virtue or one graced with vision, political or military, his biography might have provided relief to the sordid story of the conquest. This is not possible, however, when the leader himself is a source for what is sordid in the history. *"Francisco Pizarro,"* Prescott wrote in the *Literary Memoranda*, "bold, unscrupulous, cunning, cold, faithless, judicious in counsel, efficient & prompt in action — coarse — & cruel, & avaricious" (II, 166). This is the man who emerges in *Peru*. Illegitimate and illiterate, he was a swineherd in his youth in Spain. When he came to the New World in 1510 he was forty years old; he would be sixty when he set sail for Peru and conquest.

That he was bold and resolute the history makes abundantly clear. Seizing Atahuallpa was a masterful stroke, but it was marred by Pizarro's later perfidy in executing the Inca, a stain "never to be effaced on the Spanish arms in the New World." More offensive was his execution of the Inca Manco's wife in retaliation for the murder of one of his messengers by Manco's men (after having her stripped and scourged with rods, he ordered her to be shot to death with arrows). The other anecdotes and incidents pertaining to Pizarro in the history do nothing to relieve this picture of cruelty; they simply reinforce his resolute qualities.

The incident on the Isle of Gallo is illustrative. Suffering from famine and exposure, Pizarro and his handful of followers are ordered to return to Panama by the relief ship that has recently arrived. He refuses and, drawing his sword, traces a line on the sand from east to west, then addresses his men: " 'There lies Peru with its riches; here, Panamá and its poverty. Choose, each man, what best becomes a brave Castilian. For my part I go to the south.' So saying, he stepped across the line" (V, 280). It is only during his fight for his life against the assassins who have broken into the governor's palace that Pizarro gains the reader's respect. Unable to fasten his armor, he wraps his cloak around one arm and with his sword in the other fights without asking quarter. He dies with dignity after having killed three of the assassins.

In the obituary (which Prescott wrote for the important figures in his histories) he attempts the difficult assessment of the conqueror of Peru. While Pizarro possessed "something higher than mere animal courage, in that constancy of purpose which was rooted too deeply in his nature to be shaken by the wildest storms of fortune," his name became "a by-word for perfidy." After noting his subject's avarice and lack of religious principle, Prescott provides a historical perspec-

tive for evaluating the achievement of Pizarro: "When we contemplate the perils he braved, the sufferings he patiently endured,
the incredible obstacles he overcame, the magnificent results he
effected with his single arm, as it were, unaided by the government,
— though neither a good nor a great man in the highest sense of that
term, it is impossible not to regard him as a very extraordinary one"
(VII, 32).

V *"I had forgotten your face"*

If there is one feature of *The Conquest of Peru* that distinguishes
it from its predecessors, *Mexico* and *The History of the Reign of Ferdinand and Isabella the Catholic*, it is the portrayal of the Spanish
character, that striking fusion of courage, cruelty, pride, and gallows
humor. In neither of the two other histories do we see these facets
developed in the detail or depth we find in *Peru*, where there is
greater interplay between the actors. Previously, Prescott simply told
what had transpired between the actors in the histories or what was
reported to have been said. In *Peru*, however, where there are far
more personal anecdotes and quoted conversations, we seem to be
overhearing dialogue and observing firsthand the interaction
between the Spaniards as they struggle for control of an empire.

It is in their civil wars, always the most sanguinary of conflicts,
that we see revealed that strain of cruelty so characteristic of the
Renaissance Spaniard. In him the quality of mercy was not strained
— it simply did not exist. Cavaliers lying helpless from wounds
honorably received in battle are murdered either on the field or in
captivity. As for the former members of Pizarro's party, if they are
unfortunate enough to be captured by Pizarro's lieutenant Carbajal,
they are hanged immediately, "peopling the trees with their
bodies," according to one commentator (VII, 148). Yet those who so
quickly deal death to others accept it themselves with equanimity.
Viceroy Blasco Nuñez Vela, a pedantic martinet guilty of murdering
in rage a political opponent, manfully meets his own death after
fulfilling his vow to be the first to break a lance in battle. At Chupas,
overrun by Vaca de Castro's forces, Almagro's men refuse to quit the
field. "Shouting out, 'We slew Pizarro! we killed the tyrant!' They
threw themselves on the lances of their conquerors, preferring death
on the battle-field to the ignominious doom of the gibbet" (VII, 66).
There is in all of this something that inspires awe, and we appear to
be in the presence of men who are more than mortal.

In the eighty-four-year-old Francisco de Carbajal, Gonzalo
Pizarro's second in command, we find these qualities of cruelty,

courage, and gallows humor epitomized. The old soldier greatly interested Prescott, who devotes a five-page obituary to him and
provides five anecdotes for him to every one he provides Francisco
Pizarro. Consequently, Carbajal is the more interesting figure of the
two and, barring Atahuallpa, the most memorable figure in the
history. At Chupas, when the advancing line he commands falls back
from artillery fire, Carbajal, a very large man, throws off his helmet
and cuirass, calling, "Shame on you, my men! Do you give way now?
I am twice as good a mark for the enemy as any of you!" (VII, 63).
He then personally leads a successful charge against the guns. After
the victory he stays in the saddle, riding younger men and their
mounts into the ground as they try to keep up with him in his pursuit
of Gonzalo's enemies. Later, at Lima, while supervising the execution of political prisoners, he "complimented one of his victims by
telling him that, 'in consideration of his higher rank, he should have
the privilege of selecting the bough on which to be hanged!' " (VII,
115).

This grim sense of humor does not desert him at his own capture
or his execution. He affects not to recognize a commander whom he
had driven from the field more than once: "I crave your pardon . . .
it is so long since I have seen anything but your back that I had
forgotten your face!" (VII, 257). On the way to his execution he is
annoyed by a priest who repeatedly urges him to give some token of
penitence, "if it were only by repeating the *Pater Noster* and *Ave
Maria*." To be rid of the priest, Carbajal simply repeats the words
"Pater Noster," *"Ave Maria"* and then is silent.

In the depiction of men such as these who put their stamp on an
age of conquest and exploitation, Prescott distinguishes *Peru* from
his earlier histories where the representative man or woman having
his unqualified admiration directed the course of a nation or a conquest. Although *Peru* lacks a noble protagonist and unity as well as
an Indian population commensurate in ferocity with the Spanish invaders, it is still an immensely readable history. The description of
the Inca civilization, particularly its wealth, the precise explanation
of the cause of the conflict between the conquerors, and the depiction of the Spanish character — these together with the careful
research, the sheer abundance of anecdotes, and the exploitation of
primary materials all contribute to the history's continuing popularity.

CHAPTER 7

"A Pendant to Ferdinand and Isabella"

A S early as 1838 Prescott had considered as a subject for a future history the reign of Philip II, "a fruitful theme — if discussed under all its relations, civil & literary — as well as military . . . " (*Memoranda*, I, 230). In order to pursue that theme he commissioned Pascual de Gayangos to send him from the libraries and archives of Europe the rare books and manuscripts, originals and copies, necessary for a work that would be "a pendant to *Ferdinand and Isabella*."[1] By 1848 most of Prescott's collection of printed volumes and copied manuscripts on the period of Philip II were on his library's shelves, forming, according to Ticknor, "one of the richest and most complete ever made on any subject of historical research."[2] As a result Prescott undertook his last project with greater authority than he had ever had in writing his previous histories.

The collection itself, however, posed problems in the sheer amount of information it provided the historian. The assiduous collector and researcher now faced the nearly overwhelming task of converting an abundance of raw material into a polished literary record. Also, for the first time Prescott was confronted with the hard decision of what kind of work to undertake — a history such as he had written in *The History of the Reign of Ferdinand and Isabella the Catholic*, or the less demanding form of memoirs? His advancing years, his infirmities (he sometimes wrote in a kneeling position because rheumatic pain prevented his sitting at a desk), the bad state of his eye, and the amount of work necessary to complete a history ultimately influenced Prescott to choose the memoir form. He would take the whole subject of Philip II's reign, but he would be selective, treating only the most important and interesting features of the reign. "All the wearisome research into constitutional, financial, ecclesiastical details, I must discard

— or, at least, go into them sparingly — only so far as necessary to present a background to the great transactions of the reign." (*Memoranda*, II, 184)

Before he began writing, Prescott was asked by John Lothrop Motley if he had any objections to Motley's undertaking a history of the war in the Netherlands. Though it was, as Prescott wrote George Bancroft, "the cream of my subject," he encouraged Motley to proceed and offered him the use of any books in his library. Later, in the preface to his last volume of *Philip the Second*, the historian favorably mentioned Motley's forthcoming work.

By the spring of 1850 Prescott had completed two chapters of the first volume when poor health forced him to seek relief in travel to a mild climate. He allowed himself to be persuaded that a change for a while would be beneficial and agreed to visit England. It evidently had the desired effect, for, returning rested and eager for work, he completed the first volume and decided to cast the remaining ones as histories rather than memoirs.[3] The work went slowly, volumes one and two appearing in 1855. The third (the last one he completed) went to press in April, 1858, nine months before his death in January, 1859.[4]

Between the composition of the second and third volumes Prescott had written, at the request of his publisher, a new conclusion to Robertson's *Charles the Fifth* which brought the older historian's account of the emperor's last years more in line with recent scholarship and provided a more accurate beginning for Prescott's history of Charles's son. Prescott succeeds in his main purpose of documenting his rejection of the received opinion that the emperor had completely withdrawn from the business of the kingdom upon entering the monastery at Yuste. We see Charles having letters written which would not only raise money for Philip's Italian campaign, but would also indicate the places to be defended and the troops to be raised. We also witness his anger at Philip's failure to follow up his military successes and take his enemies' capitals. While there are a few interesting anecdotes about the emperor — accounts of his shooting pigeons and his ordinance decreeing a hundred lashes for any woman approaching within two bow shots of the monastery gate — the dominant impression we get is that of a gouty old man relentlessly indulging himself. Writing an interesting account of an abdication and subsequent retirement to a monastery was difficult; the most that can be said of Prescott's conclusion is that it is informative.

I *Form*

In the preface to *Philip the Second,* Prescott acknowledges the difficulty the historian faces in preserving unity of interest in a subject
that embraces "such a variety of independent, not to say in-
congruous, topics." The solution, he advises the reader, is "to keep
in view the dominant principle which controlled all the movements
of the complicated machinery . . . and impressed on [the
movements] a unity of action." This principle, he continues,

is to be found in the policy of Philip, the great aim of which was to uphold
the supremacy of the Church, and, as a consequence, that of the crown . . . it
is only by keeping this constantly in view that the student will be enabled to
obtain a clue to guide him through the intricate passages in the history of
Philip, and the best means of solving what would otherwise remain
enigmatical in his conduct. (XVI, xviii - xix) [5]

William Charvat's comment on this passage provides an insight into
the history's weakness: "It is one thing . . . to tell readers to keep a
unifying principle in view; it is quite another to use that principle
organically. *Philip II* must be read not as an analysis of a period and
a reign but as a collection of brilliant episodes."[6]

This lack of unity, in Charvat's view, stems from the history's
topical organization. Book I, for example, examines the retirement of
Charles V, the early days of Philip II, the English alliance, and the
wars with the Pope and with France; Books II and III, the revolution
in the Netherlands. Book IV, in Charvat's words, is "a mélange including a view of the Ottoman Empire, the siege of Malta, the story
of Don Carlos, and the death of Isabella." Book V deals with the
rebellion of the Moors and the war with the Turks. Book VI, of which
only two chapters were written, treats the domestic affairs in Spain.[7]

But *Ferdinand and Isabella* is also a topical history, and with few
exceptions its dramatic unity is maintained throughout. Why this,
the author's first history, possesses this important literary quality
while the product of his mature years and experience does not, is due
partly to the nature of the two histories' protagonists and their
aspirations. *Ferdinand and Isabella* (if we exclude the chapters on
the Inquisition) is the record of an age of chivalry in which a young
and virtuous queen and her consort wage and direct wars that establish a monarchy, consolidate a nation, and purge Spanish soil of
its last vestige of pagan rule. These achievements, together with the

discovery of the New World and the victories in the Italian Wars, seem manifestations of the personalities of a king and especially a queen who was an illustrious representative of the national character. We close *Ferdinand and Isabella* with the conviction that the Spanish monarchs conspired with destiny to build a new political power — a conviction reinforced by the author's explicit commentary on the significance of each of their accomplishments.

There is little likelihood that we will assume that a conspiracy existed between Philip and destiny to increase the glory of Spain. Instead we encounter a monarch who regarded indecisiveness, vacillation, and procrastination as qualities of high statecraft. In the earlier histories we saw protagonists who were vigorous rulers, decisive conquerors, or desperate brigands, but in *Philip the Second* we observe the absolute ruler of the most powerful nation in Europe making the boast (a favorite of his) that "time and he were a match for any other two" (XIX, 371). This lack of a protagonist capable of engaging our interest or sympathies accounts ultimately for the lack of dramatic unity in the history.

II *Philip II*

Philip II was neither a heroic nor a martial figure, and while this would not prejudice Prescott we must remember that his protagonists in the preceding works were all soldiers: Cortés, Pizarro, Philip's father Charles V, and his great-grandfather Ferdinand of Aragon. Even his great-grandmother Isabella had ridden in armor, reviewing the Spanish troops in the Granadine war. Given the number of wars during Philip's reign — with France, the Pope, the Ottoman Turks at Malta and Lepanto, and the Moriscoes in his own Spain — he had unlimited opportunities for personal involvement and leadership. Yet nowhere among the names linked with Spanish victories does Philip II's appear. Prescott, however, is not at a loss to explain its absence. "Philip has been accused of indolence," he writes. "As far as the body was concerned, such an accusation was well founded. Even when young, he had no fondness, as we have seen, for the robust and chivalrous sports of the age." (XIX, 362)

We are soon informed, though, that "it would indeed be a great mistake to charge him with sluggishness of mind. He was content to toil for hours, and long into the night, at his solitary labors" (XIX, 363). The direction this energy took in resurrecting the Inquisition led the historian to write of Philip in a letter to his friend Lady Lyell: "With all my good-nature I can't wash him even into the darkest

French gray. He is black and all black" (XXII, 532). While Prescott
is objective enough to grant that Philip was a sincere Catholic, he is
committed to emphasizing that Philip was "an inquisitor at heart"
(XVII, 176), and he provides impressive anecdotes to substantiate
the charge. At the *auto da fe* at Valladolid in October 1559 Prescott
has us witness the exchange between the condemned heretic Don
Carlos de Sesto and Philip: " 'Is it thus that you allow innocent subjects to be persecuted?' To which the king made the memorable
reply, 'If it were my own son, I would fetch the wood to burn him,
were he such a wretch as thou art!' " (XVII, 50). When warned that
reviving the ancient edicts against heresy in the Netherlands might
cost him the sovereignty of those provinces, Philip concludes:
"Better not reign at all than reign over heretics!" This answer,
Prescott observes, furnishes "the key to the permanent policy of
Philip in his government of the Netherlands." (XVII, 19)

Philip's evil, Prescott shows, was compounded by his personal
responsibility for the death of those Flemish Catholic nobles,
Hoorne, Egmont, and Montigny, who opposed the Inquisition for its
encroachment on liberty of conscience. After describing how the first
two were publicly executed at the King's order, the historian devotes
a chapter to documenting Philip's role in the secret murder of Montigny. Fearing the effect the public execution of another Flemish noble might have in the Netherlands, Philip contrived a way to make it
appear that his prisoner died from disease: "He at last decided on
the *garrote* . . . which, producing death by suffocation, would be less
likely to leave its traces on the body" (XVIII, 100).

Prescott found nothing in his research to lighten the portrait of
Philip. He shows him to be devoid of vision, severely limited in his
statecraft, and even for Catholic Spain, unenlightened in his
religious policies. His father's advice, "Depend on no one but
yourself. . . . Make use of all; but lean exclusively on none" (XVI,
36 - 37), Prescott shows, Philip followed assiduously. "It was a
capital defect in Philip's administration," he writes, "that his love of
power and distrust of others made him desire to do everything
himself, — even those things which could be done much better by
his ministers" (XIX, 370).

Physically inactive, procrastinating, distrustful, and because of
these, inefficient, the Spanish monarch is the least interesting of all
Prescott's protagonists. Furthermore, Philip is simply never in focus.
We neither see nor hear him enough to get that sharp impression we
are accustomed to getting of the leaders in the preceding histories.

Prescott could not find anything in Philip to admire, but unlike Motley, Prescott refused to villify Philip.[8] As a consequence, we are impressed more by the author's objectivity than by his attempt to create a memorable character.

Fortunately history compensated Prescott for the lack of a protagonist who could give unity to the work by supplying him with an impressive gallery of characters: the Duke of Alva; Pope Paul the Fourth; the leader of the Moriscoes, Aben-Aboo; Don John of Austria; the Grand Master of Malta; the Marquis of Mondejar, captain-general of Granada; Egmont; Hoorne; and William of Orange. Prescott surely intended for William to play a greater part in the history; throughout Books II and III, which treat the revolt in the Netherlands, he is clearly the central figure. In fact, the Protestant leader seems to be the protagonist of the history at this point, with Philip appearing as the antagonist who prefers to work at a great distance. Had Prescott lived to complete the history, he would have had to introduce William of Orange again, and, writing as he was from the Spanish point of view, he would have been placed in a difficult position both as an objective historian and as a literary artist. His sympathies are clearly with the Protestant cause, and his Protestant hero had already usurped the interest of the history in those chapters where he appeared. William of Orange could only further weaken the tenuous unity Philip II would have given to the history.

III   *Battles and Tactics*

The seventeen chapters covering the wars of Spain contain the spectacle, suspense, and dramatic unity largely absent from the remaining two-thirds of *Philip the Second*. Prescott was always at his best in writing military history, and in the accounts of battles and tactics we recognize his old interests and passions, particularly his fascination with innovations in armament and tactics. When the Duke of Alva crosses the Alps with his army on his march to the Netherlands, he compensates for the absence of artillery by employing

what was then a novelty in war. Each company of foot was flanked by a body of soldiers carrying heavy muskets with rests attached to them. This sort of fire-arms, from their cumbrous nature, had hitherto been used only in the defence of fortresses. But with these portable rests they were found efficient for field-service, and as such came into general use after this period. (XVII, 368 - 69)

Prescott was still intrigued by the effectiveness of the pike, whose evolution as a tactical weapon he had traced from the Italian Wars to its use in Peru. He studies it again in his account of the Spanish rout of the French forces at St. Quentin:

Amidst this confusion, the Gascons, the flower of the French infantry, behaved with admirable coolness. Throwing themselves into squares, with the pikemen armed with their long pikes in front, and the arquebusiers in the centre, they presented an impenetrable array, against which the tide of battle raged and chafed in impotent fury. It was in vain that the Spanish horse rode round the solid masses bristling with steel, if possible, to force an entrance, while an occasional shot, striking a trooper from his saddle, warned them not to approach too near. (XVI, 219 - 20)

The events that presented Prescott with the final challenge to his descriptive powers, however, were the Battle of Lepanto and the Siege of Malta, two of the most memorable battles of Philip's reign. Prescott had never described a sea engagement or a prolonged siege from the point of view of the defenders. In the Battle of Lepanto there was all the color, spectacle, and excitement a historian of Prescott's talents could desire, and he enables us to experience all of it. Three hundred galleys and eighty thousand men of the Holy League, representing Spain, the Republic of Venice, and the Holy See, sail under the command of Don John of Austria, the half brother of Philip II. From his ship, the *Real*, flies the Christian standard, a crucifix with the arms of the Church, Spain, and Venice below united by a chain from which are suspended the arms of Don John of Austria. No less impressive in its symbolism is the standard of the Ottoman empire, which, "covered with texts from the Koran, emblazoned in letters of gold, . . . had the name of Allah inscribed upon it no less than twenty-eight thousand nine hundred times" (XIX, 295). It identified the galley of Ali Pasha, the Turkish admiral commanding two hundred and fifty galleys and 120,000 men.

Prescott clearly describes the three-mile battle line, giving the number of ships and names of the opposing commanders on its left and right wings and at its center. Then, having established the respective positions of the fleets and recorded the challenge given and answered by cannon discharge, he skillfully builds suspense while creating a panoramic view of the fleets awaiting the commencement of hostilities:

At this solemn moment a death-like silence reigned throughout the armament of the confederates. Men seemed to hold their breath, as if absorbed in the expectation of some great catastrophe. The day was magnificent. A light breeze, still adverse to the Turks, played on the waters, somewhat fretted by the contrary winds. It was nearly noon; and as the sun, mounting through a cloudless sky, rose to the zenith, he seemed to pause, as if to look down on the beautiful scene, where the multitude of galleys, moving over the water, showed like a holiday spectacle rather than a preparation for mortal combat.

The illusion was soon dispelled by the fierce yells which rose on the air from the Turkish armada. It was the customary war-cry with which the Moslems entered into battle. (XIX, 291)

Prescott's account of the battle is remarkably coherent, given the scale and scope of the action along the three-mile battle line. Twice he surveys the fighting along the line from left to right, each completed traverse marking a crucial point in the battle's development. His first traverse describes the initial attacking maneuvers of the two fleets and their immediate consequences. The second begins as Prescott shifts to the left side of the line where the Venetians, after being turned by Sirocco, the viceroy of Egypt, desperately fight back and begin boarding vessel after vessel of the Moslems, eventually putting them to flight. Prescott then describes the center where, after boarding the Ali Pasha's galley for the third time, the Castilian soldiers kill the Turkish commander and run up the banner of the Cross. His account concludes with a description of the fighting on the right wing of the allies where Andrew Doria, reinforced by ships from the center of the line, drives the dey of Algiers and his squadron from the battle. For clarity and color the account of Lepanto is a remarkable performance, one that places Prescott in the first rank of Romantic historians.

Prescott's narration of the three-month siege of Malta by the Ottoman Turks and their Moorish allies is written from the point of view of the island's Christian defenders, the Knights of St. John and the Spanish and Italian troops who share with them the dangers and death of repeated assaults. As in the account of the Battle of Lepanto, Prescott's description is characterized by clarity and suspense. Geography, fortifications, and the numbers of the opposing forces are established early. Seven hundred and forty Knights of St. John, plus the Spanish and Italian troops and the three thousand militia of the island, comprise a Christian force of some 9,700 men under the command of the sixty-eight-year-old Grand Master of the Order of St. John, Jean Parisot de la Valette. Against these defenders Solyman the Second directs his lieutenants at the head of forty thousand warriors, thirty thousand of them "the flower of the Turkish Army." Because of the nature of siege warfare and the fact that two fortresses, St. Elmo and St. Michael, had to be taken, the narrative is long and suspenseful.

Prescott's account of the bloody fighting during the one-month siege of St. Elmo shows that his descriptive powers were as strong as ever when the events themselves demanded dramatic narration: " . . . and when sabre and scimitar were broken, the combatants closed with their daggers and rolled down the declivity of the breach, struggling in mortal conflict with each other" (XVIII, 197). The defenders sold themselves dearly, for 1,500 perished in a siege that cost the besiegers eight thousand warriors. In the comment of the Turkish commander on his losses, Prescott finds the perfect anecdote to conclude his account of the siege and build suspense for the Turkish attack on the fortresses of St. Angelo and St. Michael, the subject of his following chapter: " 'What will not the parent cost,' exclaimed Mustapha, — alluding to St. Angelo, — 'when the child has cost us so dear!' " (XVIII, 213).

The account of the fifty-three-day siege of St. Michael captures the ferocity of the fighting peculiar to the religious wars. At one stage we witness the slaughter of those Turks who, in their eagerness to penetrate the garrison, failed to provide for an escape route: "Some, throwing themselves on their knees, piteously begged for mercy 'Such mercy,' shouted the victors, 'as you showed at St. Elmo!' and buried their daggers in their bodies" (XVIII, 228). The losses were heavy on both sides. Prescott gives us the numbers slain and assesses the effect of the Christian victory: "The arms of Solyman the Second, during his long and glorious reign, met with no reverse so humiliating as his failure in the siege of Malta" (XVIII, 258).

IV *Persecution and Progress*

In the last chapter of his history of the Spanish nation, Prescott again examines the blighting effects of the Inquisition. Whereas in his previous histories the Inquisition had persecuted with impunity all who fell within its shadow, during Philip's reign its insistence on religious conformity resulted in open revolt and war. In the Netherlands, Prescott maintains again and again, it could not have been otherwise. Insisting on the enforcement of edicts that would deprive an individual of his liberty of conscience, Philip had failed to comprehend "the free and independent character of the people of the Netherlands" (XVI, 359). His ignorance of a people his father had understood and respected and his intransigence in regard to enforcing the Inquisition led him to send the Duke of Alva with complete military and civil authority to the Netherlands. As Prescott shows, the king could not have found a more zealous administrator. Writing Philip of the sentence of death imposed on five hundred heretics, the duke complains: "I have reiterated the sentence again and again, for they torment me with inquiries whether in this or that case it might not be commuted for banishment. They weary me of my life with their importunities." Prescott comments: "He was not too weary, however, to go on with the bloody work; for in the same letter we find him reckoning that three hundred heads more must fall before it will be time to talk of a general pardon" (XVIII, 8). While Prescott's accounts of torture endured by the Protestants are vivid, unlike some of Motley's, they are not grisly.[9] Rather, we learn of the fortitude displayed by the persecuted and its effect on the people: "On the scaffold and at the stake this intrepid spirit did not desert them, and the testimony they bore to the truth of the cause for which they suffered had such an effect on the bystanders that it was found necessary to silence them." (XVIII, 10)

In the Netherlands the Inquisition had persecuted a vigorous people who, breaking with tradition in their quest for religious and political freedom, had identified themselves with progress, a concept highly regarded by Prescott. As an heir of the Reformation and eighteenth-century Rationalism, his hostility to any counterforce is both understandable and expected. But his sympathy for victims of religious persecution was not limited to those with whom he could identify, a fact borne out by his indignation at the attempt to obliterate the Moorish culture of Granada.

In 1566 Philip signed a law the intent of which was to prevent backsliding among the Moorish converts to Christianity by cutting off "all those associations which connected the Moriscoes with their earlier history, and which were so many obstacles in the way of their present conversion" (XVIII, 407). Specifically they were forbidden to speak or write Arabic, they were to change their family names to Spanish ones, they were to give up their national dress (which included wearing of the veil in public by women), and they were forbidden to celebrate their domestic festivities with their national songs and dances. "Such," Prescott writes, "were the principal provisions of a law which, for cruelty and absurdity, has scarcely a parallel in history," and he castigates each of the main provisions: "It would be difficult to imagine any greater outrage offered to a people than the provision compelling women to lay aside their veils

— associated as these were in every Eastern mind with the ob-
ligations of modesty." The "masterpiece of the absurdity," he concludes, was the interdiction against the Arabic language, "as if by
any human art a whole population, in the space of three years, could
be made to substitute a foreign tongue for its own. . . . " (XVIII, 409 - 10)

Prescott's denunciation of the cruelty and absurdity of the edicts
establishes the presence of a moral and rational persona in the
history who holds men and institutions accountable for their vice
and folly. While the persona is primarily critical, it may also evaluate
and commend. For example, it is quite clear that we are to regard
the sack of the monasteries and burning of books and manuscripts by
the Protestant fanatics in the Netherlands as a deplorable act. "But if
the first step of the Reformation was on the ruins of art, it cannot be
denied that a compensation has been found in the good which it has
done by breaking the fetters of the intellect and opening a free range
in those domains of science to which all access had been hitherto
denied" (XVII, 281 - 82). In refusing to allow his soldiers to molest
the Moriscoe women during the pillage of Pitres, Mondejar "acted
in obedience to the dictates of sound policy, no less than of
humanity, which indeed, happily for mankind, can never be dis-
severed from each other" (XIX, 46). In this last history, as in his first,
Prescott's authorial intrusions, weighing as they do the moral consequences of events, create a tone of high seriousness appropriate to
a narrative treating the destinies of nations and men.

For the reasons already discussed, there is little evidence to indicate that had Prescott lived to complete *Philip the Second*, it
would have had either the organic quality or the appeal of the earlier
histories. Those volumes we do have, however, reveal a writer who,
despite increasing infirmity, was true to his conception of the
historian's duty and did not stint in his efforts to research thoroughly
and write vigorously whenever he could. Adverse criticism of *Philip
the Second*, then, arises more perhaps from its comparison with
Prescott's earlier histories than from flaws in the work itself.

CHAPTER 8

Style

I N April 1840, in a letter important for what it reveals about the historian's attitude toward language and his audience, Prescott replied to a letter from Thomas Stewart, a Catholic monk in Palermo, who had criticized the word choice in *The History of the Reign of Ferdinand and Isabella the Catholic.* After agreeing with Stewart's condemnation of the use of "loan" as a verb (he replied that it "should be sentenced at once without benefit of clergy"), Prescott concluded his discussion of language with the following observation: "We cannot guard too carefully against such innovations, liable to spring up in a country where an active, inventive population, less concerned with books than business, is very likely to corrupt the pure waters of 'English undefiled' in their homely every-day vocations."[1] Two inferences can be made: Prescott wrote for an English audience; therefore, he put a very high priority on correctness of language. He was more concerned, however, with the larger concept of style than with diction. Throughout the first volume of the *Literary Memoranda* and a third of the second, we find entries discussing every aspect of it — some under the formal heading of rules for composition, others in response to a reviewer's criticism of the style of *Ferdinand and Isabella.* Altogether, these entries comprise the record of an author striving to write history that would combine the literary qualities of drama, unity, and spectacle with accurate accounts of men and events in a style distinguished by clarity and precision.

I   *Rules*

Influenced as he was by his reading of the Rationalist historians and his detailed study of Lindley Murray's *English Grammar* (1795) and Hugh Blair's *Lectures on Rhetoric and Belles Lettres* (1783), it is not surprising that Prescott's style possesses the formal quality of eighteenth-century English prose and its other distinguishing characteristics and conventions: "simplicity, clarity, propriety, and precision," according to Charvat, who has examined the rules codified by Blair's *Rhetoric*, "the proper use of balance, antithesis, and metaphor" and the avoidance of " 'common or low' diction."[2] The most distinctive of the eighteenth-century conventions in Prescott's writing, balanced periods and parallelism, had appeared with some frequency in *Ferdinand and Isabella*. Assessing the science of the Moors, for example, the author concludes that "their physics were debased by magic, their chemistry degenerated into alchemy, their astronomy into astrology." (IX, 40)

The parallelism is even more formal in the account of the abortive French attempt to recover Naples: "Few military expeditions have commenced under more brilliant and imposing auspices; few have been conducted in so ill-advised a manner through their whole progress; and none attended in the close with more indiscriminate and overwhelming ruin" (X, 420).[3] These balanced sentences and rhythmic periods, Charvat points out, "like rhyme and meter in poetry, are mnemonic aids" that enabled Prescott to carry in his memory sixty pages of printed matter for correction and revision. There is no doubt that memorizing his work before writing it in its final form gave Prescott's prose an unmistakable cadence and flow.[4]

While he strove for euphony and structure in his prose, Prescott was careful not to sacrifice precision. Again the letter to Stewart is illustrative: "*Sierra* . . . meaning, as you are aware, 'a chain of mountains of a serrated form,' cannot be well expressed in English. The Sierra Nevada, Sierra Vermeja, could not be called the White Mountains, Red Mountains, etc., without losing something of their significance."[5] When General William Miller pointed out some inaccuracies of diction in Prescott's accounts of battles in *Ferdinand and Isabella*, Prescott conscientiously noted them and sent the corrections to his publisher for subsequent editions:

[For] *rampart* read "protection," Rampart only for *fortifications*, — not as here, for a *river*, — Also, they say "*scale the walls*," not "scale the ramparts." . . . *Carried by a furious cannonade* — read "reduced by" &c — they say — carried by *assault* — it means taken — but the garrison here escaped & might have capitulated. (*Memoranda*, II, 57 - 58)

At times Prescott's attempt to avoid low or common diction results in periphrasis and rhetorical flourishes. John of Aragon, when the

first view of the Moorish city of Baza before they began its siege are memorable examples. In this last, the Spaniards themselves, as though they were the figures in the foreground of a Hudson River School painting, look into the picture where far across the valley they "beheld the lordly city of Baza, reposing in the shadows of the bold sierra that stretches towards the coast. . . ." (IX, 199)

Prescott is at his best, however, in his accounts of battles, where the terrain, displacement, and maneuvering of the combatants are so carefully detailed and described that we easily follow the development of the conflict. No matter what kind of engagement — siege or sea battle, charge or retreat — he depicts all vividly, giving them drama and color by including a telling anecdote. Alvarado using his lance to vault across the breach in the causeway during the *noche triste*,[6] and Edward de Almeyda, holding the royal banner of Portugal in his teeth because he has lost both arms, are but the more striking examples.

Finally, Prescott's method of narrating a battle is ultimately cinematic, and his technique is analogous to that of a skilled cameraman. Beginning with a wide view of the opposing lines as they await the attack, he pauses for a long look at the pageantry of the scene — pennants, armor, the fantastic feathered dress of the Aztecs, the fleets of the Holy League and the Turks at Lepanto. When the battle opens, the focus narrows to one of the sides of the battle line where the opposing wings meet in the fierce hand-to-hand combat that characterized wars during the Renaissance. Then, narrowing his focus to the individual soldier engaged in his desperate struggle, Prescott creates an exceptionally strong appeal to the reader's kinesthetic sense, a sine qua non for successful battle narrative.

III *Persona*

We have already noted the presence of a strong personality behind the writing, one that expresses a point of view that is consistently progressive, rational, and moral. In all the histories the political, military, and ethical consequences of actions are explained explicitly for us and judgments rendered freely and vigorously, as though their author believed that to be merely objective were to fail one's obligation as a historian. Among Prescott's early rules for composition appears the injunction, "Enliven the narratives &c. with philosophical *reflections* &c. This is infusing a soul into your piece" (*Memoranda*, I, 51). He followed this maxim throughout his histories. The Spaniards' violations of the Moors' religious rights guaranteed by treaty represent "the frightful results to which the fairest mind may be led, when it introduces the refinements of logic into the discussions of duty" (X, 211). The Spaniards' inhuman treatment of the Indians of Peru suggests the observation that "there is something in the possession of superior strength most dangerous, in a moral view, to its possessor" (VI, 304).

Even before Prescott concluded that "great latitude may be reasonably allowed for dramatic coloring," he had advised himself in a memo: "write clearly — but do not bind your fancy down *to too strict a literality.*"[7] Without question, he was scrupulously honest in his writing; he never invented conversations. He does, however, infer states of mind and motivation; and, as Charvat points out, he provides adjectives that he could have drawn only from his imagination. For example, when Columbus describes to the Spanish court the precious metals to be found in the islands and the opportunity to Christianize the Indians, "the last consideration touched Isabella's heart most sensibly; and the whole audience, kindled with various emotions by the speaker's eloquence, filled up the perspective with gorgeous coloring of their own fancies, as ambition, or avarice, or devotional feeling predominated in their bosoms" (IX, 321-22). This kind of interpolation, anathema to the scientific historian, endows Prescott's characters with life and imparts to his work an unmistakable literary quality.

More at variance with objective historical writing than the subjective interpolations, philosophical disquisitions, and dramatic coloring is the element of humor in the histories, which, in addition to lightening the tone of the work, reveals another dimension of the historian's persona. The result is a point of view whose well-defined moral, progressive, and rational qualities are complemented by a sense of humor that is basically ironic and that achieves its most telling effects in sallies at excesses of enthusiasm, particularly as they are manifested in religious zeal. As we might suppose, the Catholic Church provided the source of much, but by no means all, of Prescott's humor. Irony of situation, wherever he found it, interested him, and he seldom resisted the impulse to comment on it.

For example, following the slaughter of his retinue in the Plaza of Caxamalca, Atahuallpa is informed by Pizarro that the Spaniards "were a generous race, warring only against those who made war on them and showing grace to all who submitted!" The Inca, Prescott suggests, "may have thought the massacre of that day an indifferent commentary on this vaunted lenity" (VI, 125). Emanuel of Portugual's banishment of all the Jews from his kingdom, a requirement demanded by his future bride, is an act "furnishing, perhaps, the only example in which love has been made one of the thousand motives for persecuting this unhappy race" (X, 110). Commenting on the deranged Joanna of Castile's belief that her husband would return to life, Prescott observes in a note: "As Philip was disembowelled, he was hardly in a condition for such an auspicious event" (XI, 116). In the notes, rather than the text of *Philip the Second*, Prescott comments on the credulity of the Catholic writers:

Tores y Aguilera tells a rather extraordinary anecdote respecting the great standard of the League in the *Real*. The figure of Christ emblazoned on it was not hit by a ball or arrow during the action, notwithstanding every other banner was pierced in a multitude of places. Two arrows, however, lodged on either side of the crucifix, when a monkey belonging to the galley ran up the mast, and, drawing out the weapons with his teeth, threw them overboard! (Chronica, fol. 75.) Considering the number of ecclesiastics on board the fleet, it is remarkable that no more miracles occurred on this occasion. (XIX, 302)

No less characteristic of Prescott's style is his mastery of the conventional devices of rhetoric, which were necessary not only to guide the reader through the histories but also to emphasize the purely informational content of the works. Transitional sentences and summarizing paragraphs that assess the significance of an event, battle, policy, or reign, while integral parts of all the histories, are particularly prominent in those having topical organization: *Ferdinand and Isabella* and *Philip the Second*, for example, where their greater geographical scope, time scheme, and multiple subjects make greater demands on the reader's concentration and comprehension. Thus it is that we find so many passages like the following, which signposting the reader's way, formally divide topics and foreshadow the events to follow: "It is now time to pause, and, before plunging anew into the stormy scenes of the Netherlands, to consider the internal administration of the country . . . " (XIX, 345); and "Before entering on the achievement of this conquest [of Granada] by Ferdinand and Isabella, it may not be amiss to notice the probable influence exerted by the Spanish Arabs on European civilization" (IX, 34).

In addition to these transitional devices, there are passages that formally summarize and assess the results and significance of an event or policy. We *witness* the siege of Malta and the conclusion of one of Gonsalvo's Italian campaigns, but we are *told* why the Turks failed to take the island and how Spanish victories increased Ferdinand's stature throughout Europe. Thus we recognize on the part of Prescott a desire to instruct that is as strong as the desire to interest and entertain. Finally, when we examine the effective presentation of Prescott's documentation, the notes and bibliographical essays, we recognize even more how closely related were his roles of researcher and stylist. That he never forgot his conception of his role as the "literary historian" is made clear from the following reminder to himself in the *Memoranda:* "*Notes.* Avoid those which are meant to piece out the text with more narrative; such notes show want of skill in the writer" (II, 70).

CHAPTER 9

Achievement

I N Prescott's own lifetime his reputation as a historian and successful author was incontrovertibly established by the sales of his books (over 91,000 copies of his works had been sold by 1860) and by his election to membership in some twenty-seven historical and international philosophical societies, among them the Royal Academy of History at Madrid, the French Institute, and the Royal Society of Berlin. His reviewers, either internationally recognized historians or men of letters eminently qualified to evaluate his work, were with few exceptions laudatory in their assessment of his histories. That their judgment so closely coincides with that of modern scholars who have written on the same subject Prescott treated and who found him a trustworthy guide proves him both a readable historian and a thorough researcher. After a century and a quarter, Prescott survives changes in the style of historical composition and the accumulation of additional facts. He remains, according to Irwin Blacker, "the most frequently published and widely sold historian in America."[1]

I *Assessments*

While contemporary reviewers, like the modern commentators on Prescott, acknowledged the picturesque and dramatic effects in his work ("sketches of scenery worthy of Scott" and "battle-pieces rivalling those of Napier," S. M. Phillips wrote in the *Edinburgh Review* in 1845 [2]), they were impressed more by the historian's accuracy, method of arrangement, and judicious and impartial treatment of his subject. Richard Ford, one of the English reviewers most knowledgeable about Spanish history, commended the accuracy of Prescott's quotations and references in *The History of the Reign of Ferdinand and Isabella the Catholic* and observed: "They stamp a guarantee on his narrative, they enable us to give a reason for our faith."[3] In the *North American Review* Prescott's friend Gardiner found the historian "as accurate as an astronomical almanac." François Guizot, impressed by the topical organization of *Philip the Second*, recognized, as had Gardiner and Gayangos in their reviews of *Ferdinand and Isabella*, the merit of departing from a strict chronological order of events in structuring a history. In *Philip*, Guizot observed, the "style of writing places the moral succession of causes above the material succession of events and supersedes, by a loftier chronology, the chronology of the almanac."[4]

Given Prescott's subject, Catholic Spain and Indian civilizations, it is not surprising that his reviewers commended so enthusiastically his impartiality and judgment. *Ferdinand and Isabella* was written "without party spirit, and without bias of any sort," according to Gayangos,[5] and Guizot noted in *Philip the Second* "the generous impartiality of a liberal mind which enters into opinions and feelings it does not share [and] assigns a fair place to diversity of situation, to disinterested motives, to traditional prejudices, [and] to irresistible circumstances."[6] More noteworthy than impartiality, if H. H. Milman's review of *Peru* is any indication, was the exercise of sound judgment while treating Indian civilizations. The author, Milman observes,

has no preconceived historic hypothesis to which he is disposed to bend the reluctant facts; his judgment is as sober as his analysis is keen; he seems to hold it the duty of the historian to relate the results of his inquiries without accounting for that which is beyond the scope of history. This is no inconsiderable praise, with the great question of the origin of Mexican and Peruvian civilization constantly before him and beckoning him onwards into the dazzling mirage of antiquarian speculation.[7]

While historians today agree with Prescott's contemporaries regarding his merits, they also concur in noting his limitations as an analytical historian. Ford, one of his earliest reviewers, made the point that was echoed by virtually every important commentator on the historian's work: "Mr. Prescott's talent is synthetical, not analytical."[8] William Sterling, assessing Prescott's work in the 1859 *Encyclopaedia Britannica*, doubted "whether his powers of philosophical analysis were equal to his skill in synthetical arrangement, — whether he could penetrate to vital principles as happily as he could marshal facts and picture events."[9] For Henry Steele Commager, writing in the *Encyclopaedia of the Social Sciences* (1934), Prescott's history "was narrative rather than analytical, descriptive rather than philosophical, and the brilliance of the coloring conceals a lack of depth."[10] While recognizing the validity of these observations, we need to remind ourselves, however, not to hold the historian accountable for something he, by his own admission, was not attempting to do, something he acknowledged in the *Literary Memoranda* he was incapable of. "Narrative history, splendidly conceived and solidly based," R. H. Humphrey's description of *Ferdinand and Isabella*,[11] is applicable to all of Prescott's works; and it is to that frame of reference that we must ultimately refer for an accurate and just assessment of Prescott's achievement.

Both nineteenth- and twentieth-century critics note the historian's strong interest in battles and leaders, his concern for the court and nobility, politics, and war, rather than for social or economic institutions. "We own that Mr. Prescott has disappointed us in his silence on the condition of the middling and lower classes of old Spain," Ford commented[12]; and Theodore Parker, Prescott's harshest critic, made the author's neglect of the common people one of the bases for his detailed argument that Prescott had failed to fulfill the office and duty of a historian.[13] To this criticism perhaps the best answer is that Prescott wisely wrote from self-recognized strength. In his study of courts and conquests, war, and politics he found the colorful threads in sufficient numbers and hues with which to weave a tapestry of his own pattern.

Readers and critics alike have allowed Prescott his subject, manner, and treatment, and the strictures of Parker were never seriously considered as detracting from Prescott's stature. In fact, not until after his death were Prescott's scholarship and interpretation seriously challenged by a group of revisionists who found his view of the Aztec and Peruvian civilizations too highly colored and romantic, a result, they concluded, of his erroneously interpreting the culture and political systems of the Indians in terms of European civilization. The leaders of this group, Lewis H. Morgan and A. F. A. Bandelier, argued in the last quarter of the nineteenth century that a closer analogy between the levels of civilization and political organization existed with North American Indian tribes such as the Iroquois. They argued the point in reviews, books, and addresses before historical associations with sufficient success to radically change Prescott's picture of the pre-Columbian civilizations and to weaken considerably, for a time at least, his reputation as a judicious interpreter of his materials.

Today, however, archaeologists and anthropologists have restored Prescott's reputation. T. A. Joyce, archaeologist at the British Museum, observed that, considering the condition of anthropological knowledge when Prescott wrote *The Conquest of Mexico*, his "fine imagination, combined with a singular sense of proportion, carried him far nearer the truth than might legitimately be expected in the case of one equipped with only the meagre critical apparatus of the period. . . . [His account of the Aztec civilization] shows a singular clarity of vision and critical balance."[14] Philip Ainsworth Means, a student of the ancient history of Peru, after assessing the charges of Morgan and Bandelier, concluded in 1931 that "Prescott's account of the Inca Empire and all that pertains to it is as good and trustworthy as any modern account, except for the fact that many penetratingly informative details have been brought forward by modern science."[15]

Today Prescott's stature is attested to by the thoroughness and accuracy of his scholarship, the artistry of his narrative, and the continuing sales of his work — an excellent test for any writer, whether historian or novelist. Since its initial publication *Ferdinand and Isabella* has gone through 147 editions and printings and six translations, while *The Conquest of Mexico* has been issued more than 200 times and translated into ten languages. In addition to their popularity, these two works and *The Conquest of Peru*, according to Roger Bigelow Merriman, the distinguished scholar in the field of Spanish history, still remain the standard authorities on the subjects they treat.[16] For these reasons, among others already mentioned, Prescott's recent biographer, C. Harvey Gardiner, concludes: "He is still considered the finest historian of the Hispanic world produced by the Anglo-Saxon world."[17]

II *Conclusion*

Setting aside for the moment the appeal of an accurate and artistically rendered historical narrative of colorful reigns and splendid conquests, we might ask what relevance or interest the work of a nineteenth-century literary historian holds for an American audience in the space age. Several answers are readily given: first, Prescott describes a heroic age, and his pages are filled with men and women who by force of their will control events. Supremely individualistic, they insist on the subordination of others to themselves, and they and their enterprises thrive as a consequence. If by chance the depiction of such characters alienates the democratic reader, it wins the reader who responds to the display of those individual and preeminently human qualities of courage, fortitude, and pride which have nothing to do with computers and agencies.

A second reason for Prescott's modern appeal is found in those magnificent battle scenes where individual heroism, gallantry, and sacrifice figure so prominently, for perhaps something of Miniver Cheevy exists in every man. There is unquestionably some atavistic strain in him that makes him respond to battles — or to their vivid descriptions. In those strong appeals to the kinesthetic sense in his depiction of sieges, cavalry charges, and hand-to-hand combat, Prescott awakens a dormant desire for participation in the action the reader sees occurring before him.

Our response to Prescott is symptomatic perhaps of a nostalgia for a point of view that saw patterns in history and a providence directing the destinies of men and nations. Each of Prescott's four histories is a narrative of definite goals: *Ferdinand and Isabella* to unify a nation; *Mexico* and *Peru* to conquer an empire, *Philip the Second*, to maintain Spanish and Catholic supremacy. Today, in contrast, nations with a sense of destiny are rare. Those that profess to have it are too often intolerant of anything less than unanimity of opinion on the part of their people. As a consequence, we not infrequently find in such nations the existence of institutions as inimical to political progress as any of those castigated by Prescott.

Moreover, Prescott also satisfies our American longing for moral certitude. There is a surprising absence of gray and ambiguity, moral or otherwise, on his canvas where heraldic colors of chivalry contrast to the black robes of the Inquisition. Issues are clearly defined; and, if we are ever in doubt concerning them, the historian himself never hesitates to score evil or probe each act or policy for its moral consequences. Although we have been conditioned today to be intellectually suspicious of moral certainties, we still long for them emotionally, and for some touchstone for sanity in an era in which language is distorted to make it flexible for purposes of persuasion. In a time when official bulletins speak of "defensive retaliation" and "protective encirclement," we find it a tonic to examine Prescott's careful use of diction and his ridicule of cant.

Finally, when the future historian of our nation's foreign and domestic policy recognizes that he comes to his task too late to invest it with drama, color, or thematic unity because styles in history writing have changed or because the subject itself rejects the attempt, he would do well to consider the example of Prescott who, while writing a splendidly conceived and solidly based narrative history, had the imagination to perceive evil and also had the sense of a moral responsibility to call it by its name. It is a precedent which has as much to recommend it now as it did when Prescott described in his first history the moral condition of another country:

The fate of Italy inculcates a most important lesson. With all this outward show of prosperity, her political institutions had gradually lost the vital principle which could alone give them stability or real value. . . . Everywhere patriotism was lost in the most intense selfishness. (X, 377 - 79)

Notes and References

QUOTATIONS from Prescott's histories are from the Montezuma Edition, ed. Wilfred Harold Munro, 22 vols., (Philadelphia: Lippincott, 1904). Volume and page references in the text are to the individual volumes identified by title in this edition: *History of the Conquest of Mexico*, vols. I - IV; *History of the Conquest of Peru*, vols. V - VII; *History of the Reign of Ferdinand and Isabella the Catholic*, vols. VIII - XI; *The History of the Reign of the Emperor Charles the Fifth with an account of the Emperor's life after his abdication by William Hickling Prescott*, vols. XII - XV; *History of the Reign of Philip the Second, King of Spain*, vols. XVI - XIX; *Biographical and Critical Miscellanies*, vols. XX - XXI; George Ticknor's *Life of William Hickling Prescott*, vol. XXII.

Chapter One

1. Drawing on Oliver Wendell Holmes' writings and the lives of eminent New Englanders, Darrel Abel has written a succinct account of Brahminism, in *American Literature: Literature of the Atlantic Culture* (Great Neck, N.Y., 1963), II, 266 - 76. I am indebted to him for this composite picture of the New England aristocracy.

2. Holmes, *Elsie Venner*, Standard Library Edition (Boston, 1892), V, 4.

3. George Ticknor, *Life of William Hickling Prescott*, Montezuma Edition, Appendix A, "The Prescott Family," vol. XXII. This standard life of Prescott was written by his lifelong friend. Other useful biographies are Rollo Ogden, *William Hickling Prescott*, American Men of Letters Series (Boston, 1904); Harry Thurston Peck, *William Hickling Prescott*, English Men of Letters Series (New York, 1926); and C. Harvey Gardiner, *William Hickling Prescott, A Biography* (Austin, Tex., 1969).

4. Of the seven children born to the Prescotts, only three survived infancy: William, Catherine (1799 - 1864), and Edward Goldsborough, editor, lawyer, and Episcopal clergyman (1804 - 1844).

5. Ticknor, *Life*, XXII, 181, 72 - 73.

6. Prescott contributed three items to the *Club-Room*, a lead article denying the magazine's attempt to imitate the *Salmagundi Papers* and two sentimental tales, "Calais" (March 1820) and "The Vale of Alleriot" (April 1820).

7. C. Harvey Gardiner, ed., *The Papers of William Hickling Prescott* (Urbana, Ill. 1964), p. 22.

8. Ticknor, *Life*, XXII, 79.

9. Gardiner, ed., *Papers*, p. 40.

10. C. Harvey Gardiner, ed., *The Literary Memoranda of William Hickling Prescott*, 2 vols. (Norman, Okla., 1961), I, 23 - 24, 44 - 45. All subsequent references in the text are abbreviated *Memoranda*.

11. Ticknor, *Life*, XXII, 96.

12. Gardiner, ed., *Papers*, p. 40.

13. Roger Wolcott, ed., *The Correspondence of William Hickling Prescott, 1833 - 1847* (Boston, 1925), p. 590.

14. Rollo Ogden, *William Hickling Prescott*, American Men of Letters Series (Boston, 1904), p. 83.

15. Wolcott, ed., *Correspondence*, p. 648.

16. *Ibid.*, p. 3.

17. Ticknor, *Life*, XXII, 467.

18. Wolcott, ed., *Correspondence*, pp. 71 - 72.

19. William Charvat and Michael Kraus, eds., *William Hickling Prescott: Representative Selections*, American Writers Series (New York, 1943), p. xxxvii.

20. Gardiner, ed., *Papers*, p. 116.

21. Ticknor, *Life*, XXII, 333.

22. *Ibid.*, XXII, 181.

23. In 1845 Prescott, at the request of his British publisher, Bentley, prepared a volume of the essays and reviews he had written over the past twenty years for the *North American Review*. The American edition, *Biographical and Critical Miscellanies* (1845), revised and enlarged in 1850, contains fourteen essays ranging from literary history ("Italian Narrative Poetry" and "Cervantes") to detailed examinations of works by Prescott's friends (Ticknor's *History of Spanish Literature* and Bancroft's *United States*).

The critical consensus of the *Miscellanies* is that it is undistinguished. Had Prescott not earlier made his reputation as the historian of Ferdinand and Isabella and the conquest of Mexico, it would have had no market. The pieces reveal the breadth of Prescott's studies and can be read profitably for his ideas of historical composition, but, in Rollo Ogden's words, we turn in vain to them "for real criticism, deep insight into literature or life, [or] vigorous comment." See Ogden, pp. 63 - 71; Gardiner, *William Hickling Prescott, A Biography*, pp. 240 - 42; and Charvat, "Prescott as Literary Critic," in Charvat and Kraus, *William Hickling Prescott*; pp. lxxxviii - ci.

Chapter Two

1. For discussions of the interest in the Spanish subject at the time of Prescott's entry into the field of Spanish history, see Stanley T. Williams, *The Spanish Background of American Literature*, 2 vols. (New Haven, 1955); and Charvat and Kraus, eds., *Prescott*, pp. xxx - xxxvi. For discussions

of Prescott's research and methods of composition see Ticknor, *Life*, XXII; C. Harvey Gardiner, *Prescott;* and Charvat and Kraus, eds., *Prescott*, pp. xlviii - lxiii. See also Gardiner, ed., *Literary Memoranda*.

2. Williams, *Spanish Background*, I, 18.

3. For an estimate of Robertson see Harry Elmer Barnes, *A History of Historical Writing* (Norman, Okla., 1937), pp. 156 - 58; and W. H. Allison et al., eds., *A Guide to Historical Literature* (New York, 1931), pp. 337, 1065.

4. Gardiner, ed., *Papers*, p. 55.

5. These purchases did not consist of a few titles but involved long lists of works: eighty-two items purchased December 18, 1826, thirty items purchased December 30, 1826. See Williams, *Spanish Background*, II, 316.

6. See C. Harvey Gardiner, "Prescott's Most Valuable Aide: Pascual de Gayangos," *William Hickling Prescott: A Memorial*, eds. Howard F. Cline, C. Harvey Gardiner, and Charles Gibson, *Hispanic American Historical Review* centennial issue (Durham, N. C., 1959), pp. 81 - 115.

7. This was one of the more interesting tasks performed by Gayangos. "Sir Thomas," he wrote Prescott, "owns over 12,000 manuscripts, for the most part in boxes, or in closets and outhouses and even under his own bed; he does not know himself what he has and it would not be an easy task to find a few selected from his catalogue. Moreover on the very day of my arrival at Broadways his oldest daughter who had been having a love affair with a young man named Hallywell eloped with him to Brighton where they have since married, so that with looking for manuscripts and mourning the loss of his daughter poor Sir Thomas had his hands full." Wolcott, ed., *Correspondence*, pp. 314 - 15.

8. Wolcott, ed., *Correspondence*, p. 151.

9. See Williams, *Spanish Background*, II, 314.

10. Gardiner, ed., *Literary Memoranda*, II, 120, 160, 162 - 63.

11. Gardiner writes in *Prescott, A Biography*, p. 86: "Prescott's vision fluctuated, but not as some writers suggest. Back and forth, across the years, William's sight generally ranged from good to fair to poor, not from poor to nonexistent." Gardiner credits Prescott for his physical triumph over indolence and social appetites, not blindness (pp. 210 - 12).

12. For the names of the reader-secretaries see Ticknor, *Life*, XXII, 110.

13. Gardiner, ed., *Papers*, p. 47.

Chapter Three

1. Wolcott, ed., *Correspondence*, p. 107.

2. The essay, entitled "Historical Composition," had appeared in the *North American Review*, XXIX (October 1829). It was reprinted as "Irving's Conquest of Granada" in the *Biographical and Critical Miscellanies*, XX, 89ff.

3. For a discussion of Prescott's theory of history and the influences on it, see Ticknor, *Life*, XXII; Gardiner, *Prescott, A Biography;* Charvat and Kraus, eds., "Introduction," *Prescott;* Harry Elmer Barnes, *A History of Historical Writing* (Norman, Okla., 1937); and David Levin, *History as*

Romantic Art: Bancroft, Prescott, Motley, and Parkman (Stanford, Cal., 1959). Prescott's own comments in the *Literary Memoranda* are invaluable.

4. Review of Irving's *Conquest of Granada* in *Biographical and Critical Miscellanies*, Montezuma Edition of *The Works of William Hickling Prescott*, 22 vols.(Philadelphia, 1904), XX, 97.

5. *Ibid.*, XX, 98.

6. *Ibid.*, XX, 105.

7. *Ibid.*, XX, 105.

8. Barnes, *Historical Writing*, pp. 178 - 80. Although Barnes is critical of what he calls the "semi-obscurantic tendencies" and "the philosophical vagaries" of the school, he credits the Romanticists for having a "broader, sounder, and more truly historical conception of cultural and institutional development than the Rationalist historians as a group." (p. 180)

9. Barnes, *Historical Writing*, p. 183.

10. Prescott had read Sharon Turner, the English historian who, according to Barnes, p. 184, "eulogized the rude Anglo-Saxons and contrasted them with the decadent Romans whom they superseded."

11. Levin, *History as Romantic Art*, pp. 24 - 25.

12. *Biographical and Critical Miscellanies*, XX, 290.

13. *Ibid.*, XX, 294.

14. Levin, *History as Romantic Art*, p. 94.

15. Review of Bancroft's *United States* in *Biographical and Critical Miscellanies*, XX, 294 - 96.

16. *Ibid.*, XX, 302 - 303. The *Literary Memoranda*, I, 83 - 84, shows Prescott reading volumes IX and XVI in the early months of 1827.

17. Review of Irving's *Conquest of Granada*, XX, 100.

18. Levin, *History as Romantic Art*, p. 14.

19. *Ibid.*, p. 50.

20. *Conquest of Mexico*, Montezuma Edition, I, 325.

21. *Ibid.*, I, 330.

22. *Ibid.*, III, 213 - 15.

23. Levin, *History as Romantic Art*, p. 73.

24. "Sir Walter Scott," in *Biographical and Critical Miscellanies*, XX, 280.

25. *Ibid.*, XX, 282 - 83.

26. Review of Irving's *Conquest of Granada*, XX, 108.

27. Wolcott, ed., *Correspondence*, p. 140.

28. Ticknor, *Life*, XXII, 249.

29. *Ibid.*, 271.

30. *Ibid.*, 469.

31. Review of Bancroft's *United States*, XX, 321 - 23.

Chapter Four

1. *History of the Reign of Ferdinand and Isabella the Catholic*, Montezuma Edition, ed. Wilfred Harold Munro, vols. VIII - XI (Philadelphia, 1904). Citations in the text are to this edition.

2. For important reviews of the history see W. H. Gardiner in *North*

American Review, XLVI (January 1838), 203 - 91; Richard Ford in *Quarterly Review*, LXIV (June 1839), 1 - 58; and Pascual de Gayangos in *Edinburgh Review*, LXVIII (January 1839), 199 - 214.

3. This correlation between geography and moral vigor appears again in Prescott's discussion of Barcelona: "The sea-board would seem to be the natural seat of liberty. There is something in the very presence, in the atmosphere of the ocean, which invigorates not only the physical but the moral energies of man. The adventurous life of the mariner familiarizes him with dangers, and early accustoms him to independence" (VIII, 63).

4. *Literary Memoranda*, I, 94 - 95.

5. He developed this concept in some detail in the history. See, for example, X, 377 - 79.

6. Gayangos, *Edinburgh Review*, LXVIII (January 1839), 213, notes: "Still, good as her intentions may have been, Isabella must always be considered as the principal instrument in the establishment of the Inquisition."

7. William Hickling Prescott, *History of the Reign of Ferdinand and Isabella the Catholic*, ed. C. Harvey Gardiner (Carbondale, Ill., 1962), p. 10. Gardiner, commenting on the ratio of the notes to the text, observes that some of the notes were of questionable value. He found Prescott duplicating on occasion the sense or exact words rendered in the text by offering it anew in the original language in the notes. If Prescott did overdo his documentation, Gardiner concedes that "none the less *Ferdinand and Isabella* represents an historiographical watershed in America, betokening as it does a new standard of authoritative excellence."

Chapter Five

1. Wolcott, ed., *Correspondence*, p. 32.

2. *Ibid.*, p. 421.

3. For important reviews of the work see H. H. Milman in *Quarterly Review*, LXXIII (December 1843), 187 - 235; S. M. Phillips in *Edinburgh Review*, LXXXI (April 1845), 228 - 49; and Theodore Parker in *Massachusetts Quarterly Review*, II (September 1849), 437 - 70 (reprinted in Parker's *Works*, ed. F. P. Cobbe [London, 1863 - 70], X, 117 - 53).

4. Wolcott, ed., *Correspondence*, pp. 345 - 46.

5. In Irving's words, the act was a sacrifice: "When I gave it up to him, I, in a manner, gave him my bread; for I depended upon the profit of it to recruit my waning finances. I had no other subject at hand to supply its place" (Ticknor, *Life*, XXII, 228). For the correspondence between Irving and Prescott regarding the *Conquest of Mexico*, see XXII, 219 - 28.

6. In a note to the chapter on Mexican mythology, Prescott mentions a Dr. Siguenza identifying Quetzalcoatl with the apostle Thomas, while his own countryman, Dr. McCulloch, identifies the Mexican god with the patriarch Noah (I, 73). Of the latter, Prescott writes in the *Literary Memoranda*: "He . . . *proves* — to his own satisfaction — that the teocalli of Cholula were on the exact model of the tower of Babel, &c. &c. All this sort of moonshine may come well eno' in a professed antiquarian, and

mythological essay — but it is not history, — and my business is history" (II, 23).

7. C. Harvey Gardiner, ed., introduction to Prescott's *The History of the Conquest of Mexico* (Chicago, 1966), p. xxiii, has succinctly analyzed Prescott's method of avoiding anticlimax in the history: "As the historian fashioned his *Mexico* to avoid an early climax, he did two things: he curtailed his account of the post-conquest career of Cortés and he established the fall of Tenochtitlán [the Mexican capital], on August 13, 1521, as the end of the conquest. This latter decision does considerable violence to history, as everyone who has pursued the post-1521 career of Cortés, his captains, and his men readily knows. The widening conquest is closely related to the post-1521 campaigns of Gonzalo de Sandoval, Pedro de Alvarado, Cristóbal de Olid, and others. In truth the dramatic conquest lost its original unity of action and then shaded imperceptibly into the rather prosaic period of settlement. Prescott had no love for a disjointed story that just petered out, and so he settled upon dimensions of the conquest which do violence to it in both time and space. By abridging the conquest, Prescott's artistry triumphed at the expense of history."

8. A fifty-page chapter (I, 223 - 73) on the origins of Mexican civilization which considered its analogies with the Old World was added as an appendix.

9. *History of the Conquest of Mexico*, Montezuma Edition, ed. Wilfred Harold Munro, vols. I - IV (Philadelphia, 1904). Citations in the text are to this edition.

10. He did, however, have fifty thousand Tlascalan allies (III, 366).

Chapter Six

1. For reviews of the history see H. H. Milman in *Quarterly Review*, LXXXI (September 1847), 317 - 51; Francis Bowen in *North American Review*, LXV (October 1847), 366 - 400; and C. P. Upham in *Christian Examiner*, XLIII (September 1847), 253 - 69.

2. Wolcott, ed., *Correspondence*, p. 448.

3. *History of the Conquest of Peru*, Montezuma Edition, ed. Wilfred Harold Munro, vols. V - VII (Philadelphia, 1904). Citations in the text are to this edition.

4. In a monograph written for the *Hispanic American Historical Review*'s Prescott Memorial issue, Guillermo Lohmann Villena observes of the history: "Its distinguished place in Peruvian bibliography and its position as a landmark of historical literature remain secure today. It is a classic among works dealing with the Peruvian past." ("Notes on Prescott's Interpretation of the Conquest of Peru," *William Hickling Prescott: A Memorial*, p. 46.)

5. Levin, *History as Romantic Art*, pp. 150 - 53.

Chapter Seven

1. Ticknor, *Life*, XXII, 250.

2. *Ibid.*, 373.

3. He made the decision, according to the *Memoranda*, II, 184, when he came to write about the rebellion in the Netherlands.

4. For reviews of the history see *Blackwood's Edinburgh Magazine*, LXXIX (April 1856), 421 - 38; James Woodhouse in *Southern Literary Messenger*, XXII (February 1856), 144 - 55; and F. Guizot in *Edinburgh Review*, CV (January 1857), 1 - 45.

5. *History of the Reign of Philip the Second, King of Spain*, Montezuma Edition, ed. Wilfred Harold Munro, vols. XVI - XIX (Philadelphia, 1904). Citations in the text are to this edition.

6. Charvat, ed., *William Hickling Prescott*, pp. lxxvi - lxxvii.

7. *Ibid.*

8. Levin, *History as Romantic Art*, p. 120: "Although Motley said that Philip would not be his 'head devil' again in the *United Netherlands*, the key to his final verdict, as to his entire presentation of Philip, is the Devil. In action, Philip has been described as 'the great father of lies,' as 'more dangerous than the Turk,' as a false angel of light who 'murdered Christians in the name of Christ,' as a man whose 'malignity and duplicity' were almost 'superhuman.' "

9. On Christmas Day at the Cathedral of Tournay, Bertrand le Blas forced his way to the altar and, snatching the consecrated host from the priest's hands, broke it into bits and trampled the fragments with his feet: "A frantic sentence was . . . devised as a feeble punishment for so much wickedness. He was dragged on a hurdle, with his mouth closed with an iron gag, to the marketplace. Here his right hand and foot were burned and twisted off between two red-hot irons. His tongue was then torn out by the roots, and because he still endeavored to call upon the name of God, the iron gag was again applied. With his arms and legs fastened together behind his back, he was then hooked by the middle of his body to an iron chain, and made to swing to and fro over a slow fire till he was entirely roasted. His life lasted almost to the end of these ingenious tortures, but his fortitude lasted as long as his life." John Lothrop Motley, *The Rise of the Dutch Republic* (Philadelphia, 1898), I, 285 - 86.

Chapter Eight

1. Wolcott, ed.,*Correspondence*, p. 124.

2. Charvat, ed., *Prescott*, p. lxxix.

3. The volumes in the Montezuma Edition are identified in the headnote to the Notes and References.

4. Charvat, ed., *Prescott*, p. lxxxviii, believes that Prescott's blindness "helps to account for the exquisite articulation of his paragraphs in which each sentence has its special function in relation to the whole unit."

5. Wolcott, ed., *Correspondence*, p. 123.

6. The style of *The Conquest of Mexico* has been the subject of two studies: David Levin, "History as Romantic Art: Structure, Characterization, and Style in *The Conquest of Mexico*," in *William Hickling Prescott: A Memorial*, pp. 20 - 45; and Donald A. Ringe, "The Artistry of Prescott's *The*

Conquest of Mexico," New England Quarterly, XXVI (1953), 454 - 76.

7. Gardiner, *Papers,* p. 35.

Chapter Nine

1. Blacker, ed., *The Portable Prescott: The Rise and Decline of the Spanish Empire* (New York, 1966), p. 18.

2. Phillips, "Prescott's *Conquest of Mexico," Edinburgh Review,* LXXXI (April 1845), 229.

3. Ford, "Prescott's History of Ferdinand and Isabella," *Quarterly Review,* LXIV (June 1839), 7 - 8.

4. Guizot, "Philip II and His Times: Prescott and Motley," *Edinburgh Review,* CV (January 1857), 23. W. H. Gardiner, "Prescott's Ferdinand and Isabella," *North American Review* XLVI (January 1838), 279, observed: "Disconnected events are not detailed in exact chronological order, which belongs to the mere annalist; but are somewhat grouped with references to their intrinsic connection."

5. De Gayangos, "Prescott's History of Ferdinand and Isabella," *Edinburgh Review,* LXXVIII (January 1839), 214.

6. Guizot, "Philip II and His Times," 22. Theodore Parker, *Works,* ed., Francis Power Cobbe (London, 1865), X, 99, could not remember a line in *Ferdinand and Isabella* that seemed dictated by anti-Catholic bigotry.

7. Milman, "Prescott's Conquest of Peru," *Quarterly Review,* LXXXI (September 1847), 322.

8. Ford, "Prescott's History of Ferdinand and Isabella," 8.

9. Sterling, "William Hickling Prescott," *Encyclopaedia Britannica,* XVIII, 506. Quoted in S. A. Allibone, *A Critical Dictionary of English Literature and British and American Authors* (Philadelphia, 1897), II, 1674.

10. Commager, "William Hickling Prescott," *Encyclopaedia of the Social Sciences* (New York, 1934), XII, 324.

11. Humphrey, "William Hickling Prescott: The Man and the Historian," *William Hickling Prescott: A Memorial,* p. 7.

12. Ford, "Prescott's History of Ferdinand and Isabella," 17.

13. Parker, *Works,* X, 81 - 98.

14. T. A. Joyce, introduction to Prescott's *Conquest of Mexico* (New York, 1922), I, xx - xxi.

15. Means, "A Re-examination of Prescott's Account of Early Peru," *New England Quarterly,* IV (October 1931), 661.

16. Merriman, *The Rise of the Spanish Empire in the Old World and in the New* (New York, 1918 - 34), I, xii; III, 539, 616.

17. Gardiner, ed., introduction to Prescott's *The Conquest of Mexico* (Chicago, 1966), p. xxv.

Selected Bibliography

I. *Manuscripts*

The three major sources for Prescott manuscripts are the Massachusetts Historical Society, the Harvard Library, and the Boston Public Library. See Jerry E. Patterson, "A Checklist of Prescott Manuscripts," *William Hickling Prescott, A Memorial,* ed. Howard F. Cline, C. Harvey Gardiner, and Charles Gibson, *Hispanic American Historical Review,* Centennial Issue (Durham: Duke Univ. Press, 1959), pp. 116 - 28.

II. *Individual Histories*

History of the Reign of Ferdinand and Isabella the Catholic. 3 vols. Boston: American Stationers' Company, 1838.

History of the Conquest of Mexico, with a Preliminary View of the Ancient Mexican Civilization and the Life of Cortés. 3 vols. New York: Harper and Brothers, 1843.

History of the Conquest of Peru, with a Preliminary View of the Civilization of the Incas. 2 vols. New York: Harper and Brothers, 1847.

ROBERTSON, WILLIAM. *The History of the Reign of the Emperor Charles the Fifth.* 3 vols. Boston: Phillips, Sampson, and Company, 1857. (Prescott added "The Life of Charles the Fifth after His Abdication," III, 325 - 510.) See XV, 219 - 400, Montezuma Edition.

History of the Reign of Philip the Second, King of Spain. 3 vols. Boston: Phillips, Sampson, and Company, 1855 - 58.

III. *Collected Works*

Works. Ed. John Foster Kirk. 16 vols. Philadelphia: J. P. Lippincott, 1874.

Works. Ed. Wilfred Harold Munro. Montezuma Edition. 22 vols. Philadelphia: J. P. Lippincott Company, 1904.

Biographical and Critical Miscellanies. New York: Harper and Brothers, 1845 (revised and enlarged edition, 1850). These pieces, collected primarily from Prescott's *North American Review* essays, appear in the Montezuma Edition, vols. XX and XXI as follows:

"Memoir of Charles Brockden Brown, the American Novelist." First published as "Charles Brockden Brown," Jared Sparks, ed. *Library of American Biography.* Boston: Hilliard, Gray & Co., 1834.

[131]

"Irving's *Conquest of Granada.*" Published as "Historical Composition," *North American Review*, XXIX (October 1829), 293 - 314.

"Asylum for the Blind," *North American Review*, XXXI (July 1830), 66 - 85.

"Cervantes." Published as "Spanish Literature in America," *North American Review*, XLV (July 1837), 1 - 34.

"Sir Walter Scott," *North American Review*, XLVI (April 1838), 431 - 74.

"Chateaubriand's *English Literature,*" *North American Review*, XLIX (October 1839) 317 - 48.

"Bancroft's *United States,*" *North American Review*, LII (January 1841), 75 - 103.

"Madame Calderón's *Life in Mexico,*" *North American Review*, LVI (January 1843), 137 - 70.

"Molière," *North American Review*, XXVII (October 1828), 372 - 402.

"Italian Narrative Poetry," *North American Review*, XIX (October 1824), 337 - 89.

"Poetry and Romance of the Italians," *North American Review*, XXXIII (July 1831), 29 - 81.

"Scottish Song," *North American Review*, XXIII (July 1826), 124 - 42.

"Da Ponte's Observations," *North American Review*, XXI (July 1825), 189 - 217.

"Ticknor's *History of Spanish Literature.*" Published as "Spanish Literature," *North American Review*, LXX (January 1850), 1 - 56.

IV. *Essays and Reviews*

This list is selective. For additional items see C. Harvey Gardiner, ed., *The Literary Memoranda of William Hickling Prescott*, 2 vols. (Norman: Univ. of Oklahoma Press, 1961), I, 151, 238; and William Charvat and

Michael Kraus, eds., *William Hickling Prescott: Representative Selections*, American Writers Series (New York, 1943), pp. cxxxi - cxxxv.

"Club-Room." *The Club-Room*, No. 2 (March 1820), 43 - 50.

"Calais." *The Club-Room*, No. 2 (March 1820), 78 - 84.

"The Vale of Alleriot." *The Club-Room*, No. 3 (April 1820), 130 - 37.

"Byron's Letter on Pope," *North American Review*, XIII (October 1821), 445 - 73.

"Essay Writing," *North American Review*, XIV (April 1822), 319 - 50.

"Cui Bono?" *The United States Literary Gazette*, I (October 15, 1824), 200 - 203.

"Novel Writing," *North American Review*, XXV (July 1827), 183 - 203.

"English Literature of the Nineteenth Century," *North American Review*, XXXV (July 1832), 165 - 95.

V. *Letters and Memoranda*
The Papers of William Hickling Prescott. Selected and edited by C. Harvey Gardiner. Urbana: Univ. of Illinois Press, 1964.
The Literary Memoranda of William Hickling Prescott. Edited and with an introduction by C. Harvey Gardiner. 2 vols. Norman: Univ. of Oklahoma Press, 1961. Indispensable for insight into Prescott's aims and methods. Covers period from June 1823 to October 28, 1858.
Prescott, Unpublished Letters to Gayangos in the Library of The Hispanic Society of America. Edited with notes by Clara Louisa Penney. New York: Hispanic Society of America, 1927.
The Correspondence of William Hickling Prescott, 1833 - 1847. Transcribed and edited by Roger Wolcott. Boston and New York: Houghton Mifflin, 1925.

SECONDARY SOURCES

I. *Biography*
GARDINER, C. HARVEY. *William Hickling Prescott, A Biography.* Austin: Univ. of Texas Press, 1969. Draws on the historian's papers which were largely neglected by his earlier biographers, Ticknor, Ogden, and Peck. An indispensable reference work for the student of Prescott, it relates the man to his age and traces his development as a historian.

OGDEN, ROLLO. *William Hickling Prescott*. American Men of Letters Series. Boston and New York: Houghton Mifflin, 1904. Accurately assesses the limitations of Prescott's literary criticism; contrasts his approach to criticism with that of James Russell Lowell.

PECK, HARRY THURSTON. *William Hickling Prescott*. English Men of Letters Series. New York: Macmillan, 1926. Valuable for comments on the individual histories and Prescott's style.

TICKNOR, GEORGE. *Life of William Hickling Prescott*. Boston: Ticknor and Fields, 1864. (Vol. 22 of the Montezuma Edition, Vol. 16 of the 1874 collected *Works* edited by Kirk.) Warm, uncritical portrait of the historian by his lifelong friend; still the best "life" of Prescott.

II. *Bibliography*

CHARVAT, WILLIAM, and MICHAEL KRAUS, eds. *William Hickling Prescott: Representative Selections, with Introduction, Bibliography, and Notes*. New York: American Book Company, 1943, pp. cxxxi - cxlii. The most comprehensive bibliography of Prescott. Should be supplemented with Gardiner's biography for unlisted items.

GARDINER, C. HARVEY. *William Hickling Prescott: An Annotated Bibliography of Published Works*. Hispanic Foundation Bibliographical Series, No. 4. Washington: Library of Congress, 1958. Locates and describes copies of every issue of the book-length works by Prescott. No listing of Prescott's uncollected pieces or criticism of the historian.

III. *Historical and Intellectual Backgrounds, Criticism, and Reviews*

ABEL, DARREL. *American Literature: Literature of the Atlantic Culture*, vol. II. Great Neck, N.Y.: Barron's Educational Series, Inc., 1963. Entertaining, succinct account of the Brahmin caste of New England; critical of its parochialism and indifference to needed social reform.

ALLIBONE, S. A. *A Critical Dictionary of English Literature and British and American Authors*. Philadelphia: J. P. Lippincott Company, 1858 - 71, II, 1663 - 75. Assessments of Prescott by other historians. Contains excerpts from contemporary reviews of his histories.

BARNES, HARRY ELMER. *A History of Historical Writing*. Norman: Univ. of Oklahoma Press, 1937. Excellent introduction to the Rationalist and Romanticist historians. Comments on many historians who influenced Prescott.

CHARVAT, WILLIAM, and MICHAEL KRAUS, eds. *William Hickling Prescott, Representative Selections, with Introduction, Bibliography, and Notes*. New York: American Book Company, 1943. Basic reference work for Prescott. An excellent introduction and comprehensive bibliography.

CLINE, HOWARD F., C. HARVEY GARDINER, and CHARLES GIBSON, eds. *William Hickling Prescott: A Memorial. The Hispanic American Historical Review*, Centennial Issue. Durham: Duke Univ. Press, 1959. Essays on Prescott by specialists in Hispanic-American history.

Includes contemporary reviews of the four histories and a study of the style of *The Conquest of Mexico.*

FORD, RICHARD. "Prescott's History of Ferdinand and Isabella." *Quarterly Review,* LXIV (June 1839), 1 - 58. A careful assessment of Prescott's first history by the English reviewer most knowledgeable about Spain.

GARDINER, C. HARVEY, ed. *History of the Conquest of Mexico* by William Hickling Prescott (abridged). Chicago: Univ. of Chicago Press, 1966. Contains an excellent introduction by the foremost authority on Prescott; copious notes and references to secondary sources.

————. *History of Ferdinand and Isabella the Catholic* by William Hickling Prescott (abridged). Carbondale: Southern Illinois Univ. Press, 1962. Preface contains a brief but accurate assessment of Prescott's first history.

————. *Prescott and His Publishers.* Carbondale: Southern Illinois Univ. Press, 1959. Interesting study of Prescott's relationship with his publishers (especially Richard Bentley), his sales contracts, and method of stereotyping his books.

————. "Prescott's Most Indispensable Aide: Pascual de Gayangos," in *William Hickling Prescott: A Memorial. Hispanic American Historical Review,* Centennial Issue. Durham: Duke Univ. Press, 1959, pp. 81 - 115. Detailed study of the relationship between Prescott and the Spanish scholar on the Continent who gathered the materials for his histories.

GARDINER, WILLIAM HOWARD. "Prescott's *Ferdinand and Isabella.*" *North American Review,* XLVI (January 1838), 203 - 91. A highly laudatory, but informed, review by Prescott's close friend.

GAYANGOS, PASCUAL DE. "Prescott's History of Ferdinand and Isabella." Edinburgh Review, LXVIII (January 1839), 199 - 214. Important review by an eminently qualified Spanish scholar who later became Prescott's most valuable aide on the Continent.

GOLDMAN, ERIC F. "The Historians." *Literary History of the United States.* Ed. Robert E. Spiller et al. New York: Macmillan, 1955, pp. 526 - 40. Excellent discussion of the aims and achievement of Romantic historians Motley, Prescott, and Parkman.

GUIZOT, FRANÇOIS. "Philip II and His Times: Prescott and Motley," *Edinburgh Review,* CV (January 1857) 1 - 45. Commends the topical organization and the historian's impartiality. Does not rank Prescott's powers of description very high.

JOYCE, T. A. Introduction to William Hickling Prescott, *The Conquest of Mexico.* 2 vols. New York: Henry Holt, 1922, I, xix - xxxiii. Excellent assessment of Prescott's treatment of the Aztec civilization.

LEVIN, DAVID. *History as Romantic Art, Bancroft, Prescott, Motley, and Parkman.* Stanford: Stanford Univ. Press, 1959. Detailed examination of the Romantic attitudes, characters, and conventions that color and shape the work of four nineteenth-century American historians.

MEANS, PHILIP A. "A Re-examination of Prescott's Account of Early Peru."
    New England Quarterly, IV (October 1931), 645 - 62. Rejects
    Bandelier's and Morgan's view that Prescott's account of the Indian
    civilization is inaccurate. Convincingly argued.
MERRIMAN, ROGER BIGELOW. The Rise of the Spanish Empire in the Old
    World and in the New. 4 vols. New York: Macmillan, 1918 - 34.
    Distinguished work by Prescott's successor in the field of Spanish
    history. Contains brief evaluations of Prescott's Conquest of Mexico
    and Conquest of Peru.
MILMAN, H. H. "Prescott's History of the Conquest of Mexico," Quarterly
    Review, LXXIII (December 1843), 187 - 235. Very favorable
    assessment of Prescott's merits as a historian by a distinguished
    English scholar.
———. "Prescott's Conquest of Peru." Quarterly Review, LXXXI
    (September 1847) 317 - 51. Important review recognizing Prescott's
    sound judgment in his treatment of Indian civilizations.
PARKER, THEODORE. "The Character of Mr. Prescott as an Historian,"
    Massachusetts Quarterly Review, 2 (March 1849), 215 - 48.
    (Reprinted in Parker's Works, ed. F. P. Cobbe [London: Truber &
    Co., 1865] X, 81 - 117.) Carefully detailed criticism of Prescott as a
    historian.
———. "Prescott's Conquest of Mexico." Massachusetts Quarterly Review,
    II (September 1849), 437 - 70. (Reprinted in Parker's Works, ed. F. P.
    Cobbe [London: Truber & Co., 1865], X, 117 - 53.) Well-argued essay
    highly critical of Prescott's treatment of the conquest, particularly his
    failure to judge Cortés.
PHILLIPS, S. M. "Prescott's Conquest of Mexico," Edinburgh Review,
    LXXXI (April 1845), 228 - 49. Ranks Prescott's descriptive powers
    with those of Scott, Napier, and Thucydides.
RINGE, DONALD. "The Artistry of Prescott's The Conquest of Mexico," New
    England Quarterly, XXVI (December 1953), 454 - 76. Analysis of the
    interrelationship of theme, form, and character in Prescott's epic.
WILLIAMS, STANLEY T. The Spanish Background of American Literature. 2
    vols. New Haven: Yale Univ. Press, 1955. Excellent chapters on
    Prescott and early American interest in Spain.

Index

Aben-Aboo, 103
Ali Pasha, 104
Almagro, Diego de, *90*, 91, 96
Almeyda, Edward de, 113
Alphonso of Portugal, 66
Alva, Duke of (Fernando Alvarez de Toledo), 103, *107*
Alvarado, Pedro de, *78*, 113
American Stationers' Company, 24
Archivio Mediceo, 31
Ascham, Roger, 19
Aspinwall, Colonel Thomas, *24*, 72
Atahuallpa, 90, *93*, 95, 114
Axarquia, route in, 57
Aztecs, 50, *73 - 86 passim*, 87, 89

Bacon, Francis, 40
Bancroft, George, *22*, 23, 25, 36, 45, 51, 99
Bandelier, A. F. A., *119*, 120
Barante, Amable: *Histoire des Ducs de Bourgoyne*, 47
Barlow, Joel: *The Columbiad*, 28; *The Vision of Columbus*, 28, 29
Barnes, Harry E.: *A History of Historical Writing*, 41 - 42
Benavente, Toribio de, 73
Bentley, Richard, 24
Bibliothèque Universelle de Genève, 25
Bird, Robert Montgomery: *Calavar or the Knight of the Conquest*, 28; *The Infidel or The Fall of Mexico*, 28; *Orallossa*, 28
Blacker, Irwin, 117
Blair, Hugh: *Lectures on Rhetoric and Belles Lettres*, *19*, 109, 110

Blanche, daughter of John II of Aragon, 54
Brahmin caste, *15 - 16*, 22
Brahminism, 15, *18*, 21, 22, 30
Burton, Alexander, 31

Calabria, Duke of, 68
Calatrava, Grand Master of, 54
Calderón de la Barca, Angel, 32
Calderón de la Barca, Francis ("Fanny") Erskine (Inglis), *32*, 74
Calderón de la Barca, Pedro, 20
Camargo, Diego Muñoz, 73
Capponi, Marquis Gino, 32
Carbajal, Francisco de, 96 - 97
Carlos, son of John II of Aragon, 54
Carlyle, Thomas: *French Revolution*, 50
Catholic Church, *44*, 63, 64
Catholicism, 43 - 44
Caxamalca (Cajamarca), slaughter at, 90, *93*, 112
Centeno, Diego, 92
Cervantes Saavedra, Miguel de, 20
Charles V, 83, 86, 90, 91, 93, *99*, 101
Charles VIII of France, 67
Charvat, William, 100, 110, *114*
Châteaubriand, François René de, 19
Cholula, massacre at, 78
Church of Rome, 43, *44*
Cicero, 19
Circourt, Count Adolphe de, *25*, 32, 88
Clavigero, F. X.: *Storia Antica del Messico*, 71
Club-Room, The, *18*, 19
Columbus, Christopher, *28*, 29, 59
Commager, Henry Steele, 118

DATE DUE			